CONTEMPLATIVE
PRAYER

CONTEMPLATIVE PRAYER

A New Framework

DOM DAVID FOSTER

BLOOMSBURY

LONDON · NEW DELHI · NEW YORK · SYDNEY

Bloomsbury Continuum
An imprint of Bloomsbury Publishing Plc

50 Bedford Square
London
WC1B 3DP
UK

1385 Broadway
New York
NY 10018
USA

www.bloomsbury.com

**Bloomsbury, Continuum and the Diana logo are trademarks of
Bloomsbury Publishing Plc**

First published 2015

© Dom David Foster, 2015

Dom David Foster has asserted his right under the Copyright,
Designs and Patents Act, 1988, to be identified as Author of this work.

British Library Cataloguing-in-Publication Data
A catalogue record for this book is available from the British Library.

Library of Congress Cataloguing-in-Publication data has been applied for.

PB: 9781408187104
ePDF: 9781408187111
ePub: 9781408187128

2 4 6 8 10 9 7 5 3 1

Typeset by Integra Software Services Pvt. Ltd.
Printed and bound in Great Britain by CPI Group (UK) Ltd, Croydon CR0 4YY

To find out more about our authors and books visit www.bloomsbury.com.
Here you will find extracts, author interviews, details of forthcoming events
and the option to sign up for our newsletters.

Wendy Robinson (1934–2013)

CONTENTS

Introduction

God dropped out of my life one night in Oxford, as I was on my way to visit friends. It was my first term and I was desperately lonely. It was my first time away from home, and I had not faced up to how difficult, how disorientating, it was. And God was not there either. In the bitter cold, a gap yawned. A bit of solid ground I had counted on just crumbled away.

It left me terribly shocked. Explaining it away (as my friends tried to do, and it really was nothing as exceptional as all that) just missed the point. What had gripped me, for the first time, was that I could feel as lonely as *that*, without God; and, paradoxically, for all his not being there, that I could never have felt so utterly sure of God's reality – the immediacy of absence bore in. It felt like a paralysis of faith. Nothing it had given me to understand up to then bore any relation to the way I found myself that evening as I crossed Parks Road. To re-engage with God became the only thing that mattered.

Paradoxically, I knew I had to pray, and that I had to learn a whole new way of praying, where I could find God in a completely different way. I knew I had to start with that emptiness and let the sense of alienation become less disorientating, to stop still, slowly to find my way around again in the dark. It got me into contemplative prayer, and into monastic life and everything else that has followed. There have been times when it has all made some kind of sense; there have been others too, less startling than the first, back in the difficult terrain where the whole enterprise just seems absurd at best, but where there seems to be no more intelligent choice than to be patient with the sense of estrangement. It is simply, I realize, always as if for the first time. This is what the life of faith is like.

There are practical books on prayer that talk about all this. I want to explore what is involved from a more philosophical point of view. It is the question that I was asking myself back then: how can I be so sure of the immediacy of God when what I am aware of is his absence? Contemplative prayer is how we explore this question. So this book is a philosophical approach to contemplative prayer: what it is and how it is what it is.

The Christian tradition has a great deal to contribute to this, and when I first considered this book I thought it would be enough to reassert the landmarks of this tradition. However, as I began to appreciate the scale of the challenge of modern philosophy to the premises of the earlier tradition, which often focus on Platonism or Descartes, I realized that the philosophical approach I was looking for needed to address a range of fundamental questions. In fact, it would be worth exploring a new approach in order to try to reconnect the tradition of prayer with which I was familiar to more recent philosophy of religion. I was concerned that modern discussions about this tradition were dealing with something different from what I understood as contemplative prayer, but that did not seem to feature much in academic discourse. A telling hiatus. There are plenty of books on Christian mysticism, of course, many dealing with things from a historical point of view; but, as works of 'spirituality', they did not seem to address the questions I had been asking in trying to make sense of the contemplative dimension of faith.

Dom Illtyd Trethowan, a monk of Downside, used to teach that God was implicit in all our awareness. The problem is to say how. Illtyd argued strongly that our knowledge of God is not a matter of propositional reasoning on the basis of empirical experience, and the psychological categories William James used to talk about Christian mysticism also missed the point because they were essentially just about subjective states. Illtyd believed that recognizing God's presence was a matter of waking up to what it meant for a human being to be intelligently aware of things, and he was content with a broadly Platonist or Augustinian approach to explaining that.

That is the framework that has, broadly speaking, supported the Christian mystical tradition, and I do not want to reject it in this book. However, I do not think it is as accessible now as it was in the past; for a different starting point, I found myself thinking back to what was going on when prayer seemed actually to be grinding to a halt, when I was aware of almost anything but the presence of God! This made me try to rethink what was going on in the experience of prayer, as it were, without bringing God into it. The idea was, therefore, to try to think through how God does come into experience, when, of course, there is nothing in empirical terms to show for it.

The paradoxical idea of leaving God out of the experience of prayer is the kind of 'bracketing' that is characteristic of Husserl's method in phenomenology. It means trying to describe experience from the subject's point of view (as a *phenomenon*), without any preconceptions about how whatever it might be can be the object of a person's experience. The phenomenologist's concern for experience, then, is not for its subjectivity in a psychological sense, but for the way reality engages us, recognizing too that it does so in more than just cognitive or propositional terms, but through our whole way of being in the world.

Contemplative prayer is concerned with God as, in some way, the ultimate reality or, in some way, at reality's heart. And there are plenty of explanations about that, on both sides of the question whether or not he even exists. It is striking how a person who prays can somehow remain undisturbed by all the argument; even if the questions are live ones, prayer somehow works in a different way, on a different level. It engages with reality – whatever its explanation – in a different way. What it engages with, together with how that manifests itself to a person in prayer, is strange and sometimes deeply disturbing; it is also a source of fascination, sometimes of pleasure and delight. From the phenomenological point of view, it is complicated by the way the faith of the person who prays conditions the subjectivity that engages in experience, and, obviously, by the way in which the account is trying to describe a reality that is known by contrast with everything else.

This is an additional reason for my interest in the modern sense of disorientation, of loss, including the loss of meaning and of purpose – of being left hanging in the air (and in the dark): they can be places where people discover a 'call to prayer', whether or not they have the rooting in Christian practice to help them make sense of it in those terms. Some of these concerns are also represented by various styles of nihilism. I found nihilism spoke to my own sense of hollowness as well as pointing rather well at the hollowness it is possible to feel about religion. But this experience of doubt and bewilderment has a potentially religious value as a call to human growth. This bewildering place is a place of prayer. Contemplative prayer can be a way into faith; it is certainly how it grows, and how it teaches us to live forwards into hope.

The approach I outline in this book is an attempt to describe, in the experience of prayer, how God comes in. As such it has a phenomenological side to it. But I also try to reflect on the philosophical implications of that kind of account. The phenomenological side of the discussion focuses on the paradoxical experience of being drawn into something that seems empty, where we find ourselves addressed, but by a blank that, nevertheless, seems to be the essential and ultimate thing. Trying to understand that philosophically raises metaphysical and epistemological questions. Ultimately I try to bring together what I call a traditional approach and one I describe in relation to the concerns of more recent philosophical work.

Although I am not convinced by the more sceptical forms of postmodernism, its critique of modernity opens up a field where the earlier traditions of Christian thought and experience can be explored in new ways. This book cannot do much more than dip the toe in these rather deep waters, but I hope it will help the reader towards an understanding of what contemplative prayer involves and of its deep roots in human intelligence and human being.

This book is very different from the one Dom Illtyd might have written; he would probably disagree with it. However, I hope it will point to at least one way in which the Christian contemplative tradition can be approached by anyone who takes a philosophical interest in the Christian faith. I would certainly like to build some bridges to help people understand the wisdom of the Christian mystical tradition, which I do not think has always been well served by modern philosophy.

It is impossible to do this without seeing contemplative prayer as the attempt to open up a space in the heart and mind big enough for Jesus to become the central figure who helps make sense of everything. This is where the practice of prayer reaches beyond an attempt to understand experience and the various philosophical ramifications of that; at this point, what engages me with Jesus is the fullness of his divine mystery that reaches out and draws everything to himself.

I would like to thank everyone who has, wittingly or unwittingly, been so generous in helping this book reach publication. I owe particular thanks to the Dominican Priory in Cambridge where I was able to begin the serious reading and study that helped me think out the material for this book. I am indebted to the Rev Professor Sarah Coakley for the encouragement and stimulus she gave me while I was there as well as subsequently. If Dom Illtyd has been a protagonist, I must also mention Fr Fergus Kerr, OP, one of those who taught me in the Dominican Studium in Oxford in the early 1980s. He was no antagonist, but his dialogue at that time with Fr Illtyd about experience gave me my first acquaintance with Heidegger and with Wittgenstein's potential contribution to the philosophy of religion. I can hardly say how grateful I am for that. Others who, in various ways, have been sources of instruction and encouragement, to whom I owe my special thanks, include Jakob Deibl, OSB, Alison Fincham, Katharine Hall, Hayo Krombach, Andrew Louth and Hugh Walters. Similarly, I owe to the Prior of Sant'Anselmo, Fr Elias Lorenzo, OSB, the opportunity to come to Rome where I have been able to complete the research and writing of the book.

The truth is that coming to Rome has opened up a whole new area of research that would require a very different book to be written, and I am conscious of the delays that circumstances have put in the way of completing even what turns out to be this *coup d'essai*. I am all the more grateful, then, to Robin Baird-Smith and to Bloomsbury for their patience and attention to the preparations of the text for publication. But the person who, above all, helped me during the time of this book's gestation, as interlocutor, guide and Platonic Diotima, who most of all wanted to see the book but who no longer needs it, is Wendy Robinson, to whom I gratefully dedicate it.

1

Religious Experience

Prayer is not about cultivating certain states of consciousness, even though there do seem to be characteristic features when people talk about their experience of prayer. Prayer is about God. But the oddity of what a person is doing (or not doing), especially in contemplative prayer, invites attention to what is going on (or is not going on). Even though the experience of praying is not what makes it prayer, the questions deserve an answer: what is going on? How does it make sense? It is also clear that prayer, and especially perseverance in contemplative prayer, calls for mental discipline, moral virtue and attention, if only because it goes against the grain of so much of our habits and training, not to mention our impulsiveness and reactivity. This will need to be considered later on. At the outset of this book, though, I want to pay some attention to the notion of experience and to clarify a way of talking about it in relation to contemplative prayer in a way that is true to my understanding of the mainstream Christian tradition.[1]

---

[1] A useful introduction to the range of approaches, in particular to the debates between perennialists, contextualists and performatives, with good

In accounts of mystics we sometimes find extraordinary states described; there is a common tradition that these should not be taken out of proportion, and that even a certain degree of scepticism is healthy – having the experience is not the point. The more common experience of prayer is different. People often talk of dryness and darkness, of frustration, of the sense of its being a waste of time, while at the same time knowing – in a way that begs many questions even from the person at prayer – that they could not live as deeply or as truly without it. Dom John Chapman (1865–1933), whose posthumously published *Spiritual Letters* are a remarkable testimony to this kind of experience and to how to persevere in it, seems to relish the paradoxes here.[2] His famous phrases about a certain kind of experience of prayer include 'meanwhile the mind is concentrated on nothing in particular – which is God of course'; 'an act of attention to God is an act of inattention to everything else'; 'the intellect faces a blank and the will follows it'. Chapman is talking about the paradox between how it 'feels' (a blank), which is all the intellect can do with

bibliographies, is Louise Nelstrop, with Kevin Magill and Bradley B. Onishi, *Christian Mysticism: An Introduction to Contemporary Theoretical Approaches* (Farnham: Ashgate, 2009). A more far-reaching discussion is Edward Howells, 'Mysticism and the mystical: the current debate', in *The Way Supplement* 102 (2001), 15–27.

[2]John Chapman, *Spiritual Letters*, introduction by Sebastian Moore, OSB (London: Burns & Oates, 2003); also Sebastian Moore, 'Some principles for an adequate theism', *Downside Review* 95 (1977) 201–13. Sarah Coakley discusses Chapman in 'Traditions of spiritual guidance: Dom John Chapman OSB (1865–1933) on the meaning of "contemplation"' in her *Powers and Submissions: Spirituality, Philosophy and Gender* (Oxford: Blackwell, 2002) pp. 40–54, which includes the relevant bibliography.

the experience, and how we act, the commitment we make to it (the will following it).

It is easy to overlook that, for the paradox to work, the conflict in feeling Chapman describes registers a kind of ecstatic pull: the person praying is being drawn into unknown territory where God discloses himself. Chapman eschews erotic language in talking about prayer, but the erotic imagery and ecstatic experiences of some mystics at prayer do not belong to a completely different universe of meaning.[3] To this we must return at the end of this book.

Religious experience in the philosophy of religion

'Experience' is a slippery term and a number of approaches seem to me to amount to false starts. The danger is always that the experience becomes an end in itself, something that has its own significance. Having a certain kind of experience can even confer a certain status (being a 'contemplative' or a 'mystic') over the have-nots. The danger lies in thinking that you can isolate an experience either from what it is an experience *of* (its object), or from *whose* experience it is (its subject), and treat it as a kind of object in its own right as a quasi sense-datum for empirical analysis and evaluation.

---

[3]Sarah Coakley, 'Dark contemplation and epistemic transformation: the analytic theologian re-meets Teresa of Avila', in Oliver D. Crisp and Michael C. Rea (eds), *Analytic Theology: New Essays in the Philosophy of Theology* (Oxford: Oxford University Press, 2009), pp. 280–312.

Interest in religious experience in the modern philosophy of religion has often been connected with the search for arguments for the existence of God, and the empiricist frame of this interest means that much of the discussion has been based on just such a notion of experience.[4] William James is usually referred to as an example of this approach, and the research associated with Alister Hardy and David Hay into reports of religious experience shows continuing interest in this kind of work.[5] But as a basis for an argument about the existence of God, it is not at all clear how conclusive such an approach to religious experience can be.[6] A particular difficulty would be the logical step needed to identify a particular phenomenological content with God. Even if the notion of an 'ineffable experience' could be clarified, for instance, it is not thereby an experience of an ineffable being, even if that is a just characterization of God. Once it is agreed that God is not an object of perception, it is very hard for an experience-report to be accepted as sufficient evidence for God on the basis of its phenomenological content.

---

[4]Brian Davies, *An Introduction to the Philosophy of Religion*, 3rd edn (Oxford: Oxford University Press, 2003) takes a critical line; Richard Swinburne, *The Existence of God*, 2nd edn (Oxford: Oxford University Press, 2004) is sympathetic. See also Jerome Gellman, 'Mysticism and Religious Experience', in William Wainwright (ed.), *The Oxford Handbook of Philosophy of Religion* (New York: Oxford University Press, 2005), pp. 138–67.
[5]For example, the empirical study of religious experience in the work of the Alister Hardy Religious Experience Research Centre, now based at Lampeter: Alister Hardy, *Spiritual Nature of Man: A Study of Contemporary Religious Experience* (Oxford: Oxford University Press, 1979).
[6]Nicholas Lash defends a more narrative approach to experience in *Easter in Ordinary: Reflections on Christian Experience and the Knowledge of God* (London: SCM Press, 1988).

Another focus of interest has been the claim that these experiences are common to a number of religions, or to all. Besides any arguments for existence of God, then, the evidence is taken to justify the study of religion, on the basis of a 'common core' of experience, and to treat it methodologically in the manner of social sciences.

Both these interests miss the point. But they also highlight two issues that are relevant for an account of contemplative prayer. In the first place, prayer is not characterized by any specific sort of experience, and it is often very obscure what the experience of it amounts to. But a concern for the quality of experience is legitimate. Contemplative prayer is generally believed to depend on the cultivation of a kind of consciousness, of attentiveness, of mindfulness – 'contemplative practice' is a very good term for what promotes this kind of experience: indeed, the traditional wisdom in these practices is that they are the best ways of preventing prayer becoming little more than an exercise in wishful thinking or a barely disguised ego-trip.[7]

In the second place, the idea of a 'common core' experience of God carries the implication that the 'God' who is experienced in these ways is not the God of any particular religion, and certainly not the God who reveals himself in any Trinitarian way. If there is a Christian experience of God, it should be one where a person acknowledges as God the one we meet and who addresses us fully in Jesus Christ

---

[7]The term 'contemplative practice' is from Sarah Coakley, 'Dark contemplation', pp. 282–3.

and to whom we respond by the grace of the Holy Spirit. The contemplative experience of God in Christianity, in particular, has generally been in terms of an intimate personal relationship with Jesus and of the Holy Spirit. This is not what generally comes through in philosophical discussions of contemplative prayer and mysticism.

Philosophers of religion have themselves raised this kind of criticism against the approach to religious experience we have been considering so far. Religious experience cannot serve as self-evident neutral data in an empirical argument; it is shot through with interpretation and the cultural and religious contexts that ground and shape it. This is the dispute between 'perennialists' and 'contextualists', but for the purposes of my argument we need to approach experience in a different kind of way.

Experience and experiences

I want to distinguish between, on the one hand, experience as a quasi sense-datum, a psychological thing that can be counted and sorted, which therefore can be talked about in the plural ('experiences'), and, on the other, as a way of talking about things as I experience them, as they seem to me. This latter is experience as a narrative from a personal point of view. My experience of living abroad, for example, is based on all sorts of 'experiences' but, as 'my experience of living abroad', it has the form of a narrative account, discursively thought through and linguistically expressed. No doubt it will relate things I have seen and heard, the taste of the food, the feel of the heat of the sun. The narrative of all this will be the fruit of reflection that has been put into words. It will be shaped, too, by other experiences of life at home, for instance; these set up expectations (good and bad); they inform my prejudices; I make comparisons and come to conclusions.

In the experience of prayer, too, there is a story to be told. The story I told at the outset of this book is an example. To tell it involves a lot of contextual reference, not least to such faith and beliefs as I have, and the human story of which it is a part. But the distinction between an experience as a psychological event and this *narrative* sense of experience is only a stepping-stone towards the sense of experience that I think comes closest to what is needed to think about prayer. What I want to refer to is what goes *into* the narrative, if you like: what I try to put into words, what my experience is based on.

This idea of experience is what I am humanly engaged in before reflection or language come into the thinking or talking about it. The idea is elusive because to talk about it means to use language to do so. But the sense of experience I am trying to reach does not try to connect it with a wider autobiographical narrative but to focus on what is going on at a particular time; nor am I trying to isolate some discrete, psychological datum as to how it feels, which has no reference beyond my subjectivity. The sense I have in mind is how I might put some event or series of events into words, while at the same time wondering what is going on within me for it to be like that.

For example, here I am sitting at a table writing this page. What is going on in all that, not just in terms of my actions and the external situation, but including me as part of the situation? I can describe it at some length in words, but I am really concerned about what constitutes my experience of being here and doing this – what makes it the experience it is for me. To do this involves bracketing off the various levels of meaning to get at a phenomenological rather than a psychological sense of experience. As regards thinking about experience in contemplative prayer, I am concerned about understanding the relationship between the intentionality of my *praying to God* and the structures of experience that are involved when I do so. The subjective experience of prayer is of interest only in relation to that.

William James, perennialists and contextualists

William James has been mentioned as an important protagonist. In *Varieties of Religious Experience* he gave a stipulative definition of mysticism in terms of four general characteristics, or 'marks', of ineffability, noetic quality, transiency and passivity. In modern studies of mysticism, his approach has been called experientialist or perennialist, in that the experiential content is thought of as perennially constant. In reaction to it, the contextualist argues that no experience is immune from cultural, historical or religious factors. The distinction between a private experience and external context is false. It is the external context that gives mystical language its specific character and meaning. An important English representative of this position has been Stephen Katz, who draws on Wittgenstein's criticism of private language, and his view that all language has its meaning within public, social and cultural habits and practices.[8]

The argument between these two positions provides part of the background for the concerns of this book; the point that Katz makes within the terms of analytic philosophy takes a similar form to the concerns of the continental philosophical tradition that language is all we have got with which to express our thought of anything and everything. The implications and limitations of the claim that language makes the world we experience seem to me to bear closely on contemplative prayer, and on the question whether the subjective dimension of experience (at the bottom, as it were) opens onto something more, where language works in a different way altogether, if at all. But to appreciate this, more needs to be said about the notion of experience.

The argument between perennialists and contextualists has led to some important refinements. William Forman makes a powerful restatement of the perennialist position in an

---

[8]Stephen Katz, *Mysticism and Philosophical Analysis* (London: Sheldon Press, 1978); *Mysticism and Religious Traditions* (Oxford: Oxford University Press, 1983); *Mysticism and Language* (Oxford: Oxford University Press, 1992); and also *Mysticism and Sacred Scripture* (New York: Oxford University Press, 2000).

argument for what he calls 'pure consciousness events' (PCEs).[9] He accepts that James' interpretation of evidence was hasty and that there has been a change of culture in the approach to the study of religion in relation to social sciences. But he challenges what he calls an epistemological prejudice in Katz, which amounts to the view that our knowledge must be conceptually shaped; for Forman this rules out mystical experience by definition, in spite of so much evidence for experiences. He argues for the recognition of such experiences as ones of 'pure consciousness' and has tried to complement arguments advanced in the usual Western categories of the philosophy of mind and epistemology with an appeal to the witness of Zen Buddhism. To be noted, in this regard, is his reference to Thomas Merton who also studied the parallels between Christian contemplative prayer and Buddhist categories of experience. Merton took a deep interest in Suzuki's doctrine of 'no mind', as well as writing an article on Nishida Kitaro of the Kyoto school.[10]

Clearly there is a close relationship between a person's religious and cultural formation and his personal experience.

---

[9]Wayne Proudfoot, *Religious Experience* (Berkeley: University of California Press, 1985); on the other side of the debate is Robert K. C. Forman, *The Problem of Pure Consciousness* (Oxford: Oxford University Press, 1990); *The Innate Capacity: Mysticism, Psychology and Philosophy* (Oxford: Oxford University Press, 1997); *Mysticism, Mind, Consciousness* (Albany: SUNY Press, 1999).

[10]Forman refers to Thomas Merton, *Zen and the Birds of Appetite* (New York: New Directions, 1968). Compare his well-known and more mainstream discussion of prayer, first published posthumously in 1969, *Contemplative Prayer* (London: Darton, Longman & Todd, 2005); D. T. Suzuki, *The Zen Doctrine of No Mind* [1949] (New York: Weiser, 1991); Nishida Kitaro, *An Inquiry into the Good* [1911], translated by Masao Abe and Christopher Ives (New Haven: Yale University Press, 1990).

This is uncontroversial; most Christian spiritual writers do not try to argue, as William James did, that there is a core experience prior to and immune from external factors. In fact, the witnesses to mystical experience that Katz analyses for their contextual background were not concerned with the point at issue between Katz and perennialism. They were only witnessing to their experience of God in the terms they were at home with, which was naturally informed by their cultural and religious context. But the question still poses itself as to how we can account for what they understood to be an experience of God. It does not follow that the answer to this question is calling for an approach such as that of William James.

People who write about contemplative prayer and mysticism in terms of a personal experience of God, much as they distance themselves from William James and perennialism, will often seem to be very close to that position. Contextualists, however, see the way mysticism is spoken of so completely in relation to external social and cultural contexts that it is hard to be clear to what extent they would feel the need to express any commitment to the independent reality of God beyond the conventions of language. Robert Forman, for instance, calls the contextualist position constructivist.[11]

So, for a contextualist, does it matter, in the end, if God exists or not? The contextualist can seem so committed to the

---

[11]Robert Forman, *Problem of Pure Consciousness*, pp. 15–21.

claim that mystical experience originates within 'this-worldly' religious contexts that its religious character becomes a matter of comparative cultural interest, rather than a cognitive matter. Can we engage with divine reality beyond a particular culture and social setting? If so, how can experience be construed so as to account for this?

So long as the discussion is confined to meaning in religious experience, the debate over contextualism is not so important, but as soon as questions about contemplative experience become more than a matter of linguistic expression and the metaphysical question is admitted, it is necessary to distinguish between the Jamesian kind of perennialism (ineffable experiences and psychological episodes that are transcultural or independent of culture) and an account that tolerates and accepts as important the role of culture and religious specification, but which is able to assert its objective reference to God as a reality beyond a person's psychological state.

Pure consciousness

This is why the argument for 'pure consciousness events' is important. Forman wants to defend a concept of experience as awareness prior to any conceptualization in the mind of the person having the experience. This would be a concept of experience free of linguistic and contextual frames of reference and meaning. Even if we accept that our life, our belief structure, and all that we bring to our experience are conceptually organized, Forman argues that there is still something to the experience that makes it the subject of discourse, something I talk about linguistically, which is, for that reason, prior to language. That might be something, as in religious experience, that cannot be fully put into words. The traditional understanding of contemplative prayer seems to have no problem with this. The contextualist criticism of it, according to Forman, seems to reflect Kant's argument that any knowledge beyond empirical data is conceivable only because of the structures of our own minds, and the consequence of this is that cognitive contact with ultimate reality is ruled out a priori. Forman's response to what he calls a Kantian prejudice is to appeal to other sources, especially in the Buddhist tradition.

Their witness, reflecting non-Kantian contemplative traditions, is a warning of the danger of narrow-mindedness. The trouble is that Buddhist thinking is so different from European traditions that it is hard to deploy the former within Western-style philosophical arguments. Paul Williams, for example, analyses a discussion in Tibetan Buddhist thinking as a Buddhist scholar, where two lines of thinking agree that enlightenment involves a mental state that is free of conceptualization, but disagree on what this amounts to.[12] For one school, non-conceptualization is not a matter of making the mind a blank. If it could be brought about, the question

[12]Paul Williams, 'Non-conceptuality, critical reasoning and religious experience: some Tibetan Buddhist discussions', in Michael McGhee (ed.), *Philosophy, Religion and Spiritual Life*, Royal Institute of Philosophy Supplement 32 (1992), 189–210.

would be raised if it could be called a mental state at all, and how it could be distinguished from having no experience at all! Non-conceptualization is understood by this school to be a non-conceptuality that contains everything that went before. It would mean ineffability, but it would not mean awareness of something ultimately ineffable (like God or 'the ultimate').

Williams discusses the various ways in which 'the ultimate' is understood. It can be simply a state of mind in which no conceptual discrimination is going on, where a person is so absorbed in the experience of seeing blue, for example, that they are not aware *that* they are seeing blue. But it does not mean that blue is not the object of experience. In later Tibetan Buddhism, ultimate reality comes to be thought of as *not* a referent of the mind, but Williams argues that this is not to be taken literally, that the ultimate is not an intentional object of the mind, but that it is not apprehended in the way of ordinary conceptual thinking. In fact, he argues that such experiences *can* be conceptualized and that this is going on subconsciously. His conclusion is that apprehending emptiness, and uprooting our habitual mental tendencies, are only half of 'enlightenment'. It is valuable only because it uproots egoistic grasping. The point is always to integrate such awareness into everyday life so that a person can live compassionately, for the benefit of others.

Merton draws attention to a parallel between Nishida's understanding of *sunyata* (emptiness, or 'suchness') and

Merleau-Ponty. He points out that 'pure experience', before it gets analysed into subject and object, with all our conceptual apparatus, is a direct experience of undifferentiated unity, holding together as one the inner world of consciousness and the outer world reflected in it. Suzuki's discussion of 'no mind' puts more of the weight of analysis on the mysteriousness of being the subject of this kind of experience, but seems broadly to be thinking in the same kind of way.

Where does this leave Forman's idea of pure consciousness events? The people to whom he refers approach experience from a different point of view from that advocated by contextualism. But they hardly allow a restatement of anything like perennialism in the sense attributed to it in the philosophy of religion. They are exploring the contours, or structures, of experience as such, what it is like to experience something without being concerned for what it is an experience of, or what its material content might be, or what it is to have that experience. They are not talking about 'pure consciousness', in Forman's sense, as contentless experience (but 'mine'), but about purely disinterested experience ('I' do not come into it). In particular, Forman's concern with 'pure consciousness events' is to defend the possibility of knowing God on the basis of experience, free of the charge that that is only how we are interpreting things. But the people he refers to do not seem to be talking about ultimate reality in that sense at all. They seem rather to be exploring the radical structure of our experience as such. Rather than what Forman is concerned for in the idea of 'pure consciousness events', this is what seems to me to be important for understanding contemplative prayer.

A different account of mysticism

Michael Sells, an Islamic scholar, has also taken an interest in the comparative study of mystical experience. His book seems to be a strong argument for contextualists against the experientialist approaches. *Mystical Languages of Unsaying* shows that there are considerable similarities between the contemplative practices of different religions, and especially as to the place of apophaticism ('unsaying') in each of them.[13] But these similarities relate to what people do to promote contemplative experience; what they actually experience varies and is determined by the religious contexts in which contemplative practice is going on. In parenthesis, and in relation to the religious dialogue between Christianity and Buddhism, however much common ground Thomas Merton found for discussing contemplative experience, he saw the dialogue to be between two fundamentally different metaphysical traditions, not as the assertion that they were in fact the same.

Sells' work is actually a study about the practice of mysticism rather than about the contextualist approach to its meaning. In particular, it studies the ways in which language (apophatic

---

[13]Michael A. Sells, *Mystical Languages of Unsaying* (Chicago: University of Chicago Press, 1994).

language above all) shapes and articulates contemplative practice. This has been labelled a 'performative approach' to mysticism. It is not the label that makes Sells interesting but his concern for the structure of contemplative experience.

Central to his account is what he calls a 'meaning event' rather than 'experience', a turn of phrase he uses to avoid the difficulty that experience has come to be so tied up with issues of intentionality that he wants to leave open. For Sells such a meaning event is an 'anarchic moment'. It has three features: it occurs at a point beyond all willing, desire and expectation; when put into words it expresses bewilderment, a sense of paradox or contradiction, where unknowing is an essential feature of understanding; and as a performance of 'unsaying', the event is one where 'the non-intentional aspect of apophasis runs up against the concept of experience'. The conventional interface between subjective and objective aspects to experience is not properly viable.[14]

This approach is instructive for a number of reasons. To start with, it recognizes that the purpose of language is not only to describe 'things out there', but to guide practice; and he notes that language breaks down, but also that, before it does so, there is a point where it works by paradox, by what it cannot spell out – Sells analyses the subversive 'logic' of a joke as a paradigm of an 'anarchic meaning event'. He situates this event at the limit of language and of experience, where notions of intentionality, subjectivity and objectivity lose their normal

---

[14]Sells, *Mystical Languages of Unsaying*, pp. 209–15.

clarity of focus. In so far as religious traditions have similar ways of promoting access to such 'meaning events', Sells suggests a basic structure for thinking about contemplative experience, which I think deserves more reflection. His analysis suggests a structure, not only in terms of limit, but also in terms of what I would like to call a threshold of meaning. The semantic play between the Latin words for a boundary and threshold (*limes, limitis* or *limen, liminis*) is deliberate. A threshold is something that you cross: there is something beyond. But the threshold itself remains on the edge or limit of what you are leaving or entering.

Forman's contribution to the present discussion has been to draw attention to the importance of thinking about a kind of experience that runs counter to the sort of assumptions we make about experience in a post-Kantian and empirical worldview. Contemplative experience goes against the grain of these assumptions. Sells' work suggests that the task is to think about the structure of experience; religious experience may be less a matter of *what* we experience as about *how* we experience, and in particular that to understand experience in terms of an experience of God will not be a simple matter of talking in terms of either perennialism or contextualism.

Thresholds of experience

The experience in Oxford that got me thinking about contemplative prayer is far from what would be called a mystical experience. It was a decidedly ordinary one, which hit me rather than grew as the fruit of sustained spiritual practice. But it shares some of the characteristics of what I think of as mystical experience in so far as it involves reaching a limit of understanding. It is an existential kind of thing. In the Introduction, I mentioned that many people, with or without faith, seem to find themselves in borderlands or on edges of experience, in the metaphorical world of limits, or *liminality*. The relevant feature is that a limit is reached, which can be a threshold to a different kind of awareness. Thresholds of experience, then, are not only the 'high points' that are often the kind of thing that get into anthologies of mystical experience; they can be times of brute loss and confusion. They can be good or bad experiences, felt in terms of light or dark. Furthermore, a limit experience for one person will not be the same for another, nor will it always be a threshold.

It would be ridiculous to suppose there was an exhaustive list, but the following are kinds of experience that I think can give a better idea of what I have in mind. Some of them will be familiar from people's accounts of heightened awareness, in 'peak moments'. They may indeed include a sense of 'communion' with something ultimate or just greater. People also talk of 'go with the flow' moments where there is a similar sense of individuality merging with a greater whole, though without loss of identity. There are shock experiences that serve as wake-up calls. Conversion experiences are a particularly relevant example of these. There are also the tougher, darker times – the experience of being held as a hostage, or the torture of solitary confinement with the ever-present threat of madness.

Limits are found not only at extremes like these. The boring ordinariness of things is where people usually practise contemplative prayer, where there is therefore a way of exploring the edge of life. It is why 'desert spirituality' seems to speak to contemporary experience as eloquently as it does. Connected to it are the various blanks and metaphorical brick walls people face, where there is an immovable issue or a sense of fruitlessness, loss of direction, motivation or that sort of thing. To paraphrase a description of the sort of experience in prayer where the *Book of Privy Counselling* is trying to give help: there is just the sense of being there aware, as it were, of just the hardness of the chair and an empty stomach, ready to turn the mind and heart to anything else but God.[15]

Thinking about these kinds of experience, both in my own case as well as in reading and listening to the experiences of others, what strikes me is not the content of the experience but rather what is going on in the person having it (not the *what* but the *how*). A preliminary consideration suggests reflections such as these:

- There is a sense of being overwhelmed. We have expressions like 'breathtaking', 'riveting', 'stunned'. What strikes me is the sense of loss of control; I cannot take

---

[15]See *Book of Privy Counselling*, ch. 1, in A. C. Spearing (trans. with intro. and notes), *The Cloud of Unknowing and Other Works* (London: Penguin Books, 2001).

things in, I don't know how to respond, to relate to what is going on. The experience can go in different ways, either taking me out of myself, or forcing me back into myself, but always conveying a sense of inadequacy. In terms of a standard model of perception (where I know where I am and how to manage a situation), the subject–object relationship is thrown out of its usual balance. Classical rhetoric would talk in terms of the 'sublime'. In *The Idea of the Holy* (1917), Rudolf Otto talked of the 'holy' as the *mysterium tremendum et fascinans* – the sense of being caught up in something larger than life, and all-encompassing (*mysterium*), which causes a physical sense of fear or trembling (*tremendum*) but which is also compelling, alluring, and is in some way taking command of my will (*fascinans*). He is typically placed with James among perennialists, but the interest of his study is, I think, rather its focus on the *how* question.

- The experience may be the result of an excess of information that needs to be taken in, or of an absence of sensory input; sense deprivation, like silence, which can heighten alertness and sensitivity, can also be too much to bear.

- The perceptual limits can be reached either in a single moment or over a period of time. In a similar way to the effect of flashing lights on someone who is epileptic, a series of strong but disjointed events, which a person is unable to connect and make sense of, can cause a state of shock. Where it is a matter of deprivation rather than excess, a sudden bereavement can be as devastating a loss as the gradual seepage of meaning that leads someone over a long period of time into depression.

- So far I have thought mainly in terms of the limits of what I am able to take in perceptually. But there clearly is an emotional side to this as well. Making sense of my experience involves emotional capacities; emotional intelligence can be taken to the limit where I simply do not know how to engage emotionally, and I lose control of them. They can turn out to be paradoxical responses, along the lines of weeping for joy; but it can also be a kind of numbness – emotional responses just shut down, at least temporarily, as in a state of shock.

- Not far removed from the question of responsiveness, inevitably, is the dimension of what should be done. Again the patterns of judgement I have learned, but which have been disrupted in a limit experience, are not so readily available. I can be paralysed by fear, but also by more complex forms of emotional response. A person becomes extremely vulnerable to suggestion at these points, as anyone trained in techniques of interrogation or torture knows.

- The outcome of this is that my characteristic ways of understanding myself, of identifying myself in distinction to anything else, is disrupted. This crisis of identity or individuality can result in a sense of communion or of going outside myself in a state of deeper union. This can be experienced as a stable condition or as a fluid one, of 'going with the flow'.

These are what seem to me characteristics of what might be called *liminal* states. The point is not the psychological description that William James was interested in. It is that in conditions like these we find that we have reached a limit or a threshold. The psychological dimension needs to be bracketed off as well as the circumstances that govern the way it all feels. Then we can try to understand that there is a structure that is implicit in all our experience, that there is a way of experiencing things that can be non-conceptual, or at least prior to conceptualization, or where any conceptualization we bring to the having of the experience is contingent on the way we actually come to understand what is going on. This is the way I think it may be possible to think about contemplative experience in religious terms as an encounter with God.

2

A Traditional Framework

In Chapter 1, I set out to describe a field of experience that I think is fundamental to contemplative prayer. I called it liminal experience, a term which refers to the structure implicit in the experience, not what has occasioned it or what it is of; I claimed that there are paradigm kinds of event that disclose this structure. What distinguishes liminal experience is that our usual way of relating cognitively to things is disrupted. I do not engage with it in the usual way as subject to object. But that can allow a new kind of engagement to emerge, a shift, as I put it, from a limit to a threshold.

How I respond to liminal experience will depend on the framework I bring to understanding my experience, although it is not the framework that constitutes the experience. What has interested me in writing this book is the idea that a traditional framework, which many people who have been taught contemplative prayer will recognize, but which (for better or worse) has run up against various philosophical objections, would perhaps be better understood if it were re-evaluated in relation to a different framework, which in its turn tries to respond to those objections.

In making this link between contemplative prayer and the structure of human experience, I do not presuppose that a Christian faith commitment is implicit in human experience. However, we engage with experience on the basis of some fundamental epistemological commitments. As will become clear, and as Wittgenstein argues in *On Certainty*, there are fundamental or grounding beliefs, with a rational status and function of their own, which rely on underlying attitudes to human life similar to faith. This is why I distinguish between a human being's capacity for contemplative experience and Christian contemplative prayer. In making this distinction, I am also inclined to think that, where we can talk about faith in a neutral sense without explicitly religious commitments, there is a complementary sense in which we can talk about hope, and even love. The triple scheme has been heavily influenced by St Paul and the Christian theological tradition, but I think the three go together as human categories with which we can appreciate what is going on when people find themselves engaging with liminal experience as a place of faith.

The Christian understanding of contemplative prayer and the practices that go with it are the stuff of a large number of books, practical and historical, aimed at scholarly as well as very ordinary readerships. It would be otiose to add to the bibliography, and this chapter only seeks to synthesize their approach, and to consider the issues that have arisen from it in relation to the possibility of a new one.[1] My concern is, as I explained in the Introduction, that it is not a tradition that speaks with much authority outside the field of spirituality and (especially historical) theology; it has lost its anchorage in the philosophical culture it once had. And, in particular, it does not start where I think many people nowadays hear the call to prayer (but often without appreciating it) in the questions about meaning that surface, for instance, in the experience of postmodernity with its implicit nihilism.

As a general approach to spirituality or mysticism, I think the tradition reflects to a greater or lesser extent what has been called a Platonist tradition, with all apologies due to more fastidious scholars.[2] The story is obviously more sophisticated than that, and there was an evident growth in the theological autonomy of Christian thinking, especially as the implications of faith in the incarnation were worked out in Trinitarian doctrine and anthropology. In its early period especially, the tradition belongs to a general philosophical culture of the period. This philosophical tradition is the sort of grounding for thinking and living that, when it is challenged and dismantled

---

[1]Bernard McGinn's trilogy is a point of reference: *The Foundations of Mysticism: Origins to the Fifth Century*, The Presence of God: A History of Western Christian Mysticism (New York: Crossroad, 1991); *The Growth of Mysticism* (New York: Crossroad, 1994); *The Flowering of Mysticism: Men and Women in the New Mysticism (1200–1350)* (New York: Crossroad, 1998). See also Bernard McGinn, 'Quo vadis? Reflections on the current study of mysticism', *Christian Spirituality* 6: 1 (1998), 13–21.

[2]The Platonist background of the early period is highlighted in a classic treatment by Andrew Louth, *Origins of the Christian Mystical Tradition: From Plato to Denys*, 2nd edn (Oxford: Oxford University Press, 2007).

in the early modern period, leaves the kind of philosophical emptiness that comes to be called nihilism. This is the broad context in which this chapter seeks to look at some of the issues raised by the contemplative tradition.

Context of the contemplative tradition

Some general observations about the tradition can be made to start with. To some extent they relate to the argument between perennialists and contextualists touched on in the last chapter. Contextualists make a great deal of the fact that this tradition is heavily informed by a literary, cultural, liturgical tradition of Christianity, and certainly in the past it was easy to overlook the extent to which these contextual elements shaped the teaching and the experience that is reported in the literature of this tradition.[3] But the cultural material is all we have. This gives contextualism an unfair advantage in the debate. It is one thing to talk about the Christian experience of faith, either as an ancient commentator, like St Ambrose or St Gregory of Nyssa, or as a modern scholar of their writings; but it is another actually to pray. The contemporaries of Ambrose or Gregory may or may not have been able to identify with their kind of philosophical and theological *account*, and we have no reason

---

[3]Benedetto Calati, 'Western mysticism', *Downside Review* 98 (1980), 201–13; Rowan Williams, 'Butler's Western mysticism: towards an assessment', *Downside Review* 102 (1984), 197–215.

to expect that it is an account of *their experience*. It is the way their bishops talked about it.[4]

An example of how *different* ordinary people's experience was from a theological style of account is given in the sad story of Abba Serapion. In AD 399 the Patriarch of Alexandria, Theophilus, tried to enforce the intellectualist theology of Origen on monks who did not have the classical culture of the city. Abba Serapion was presumably not the only one to be upset: 'Woe is me! They have taken my God from me and I have none to grasp. Nor do I know whom I should adore or address.' The saying survives, ironically, because it is transmitted in the discourse of Abba Isaac on prayer, who represented the other tradition of prayer. He was amazed how even such a holy man as Serapion could have been deluded by the Evil One.[5]

For all the difference between Serapion and Isaac as to their understanding of God, their experience and their practice of prayer are likely to have been similar. That is to say, from day to day they were likely to have had similar routines and to have had to deal with the same struggles in prayer as anyone else. But different frameworks were being used to understand it, and to misunderstand each other. And neither would have seen the problem between them as one between

---

[4]For an insight of how the practice of prayer in the early period can seem strange to one who is familiar only with the theological and exegetical texts of that time, see Gabriel Bunge, *Earthen Vessels: The Practice of Personal Prayer According to the Patristic Tradition* (San Francisco: Ignatius Press 2002).
[5]John Cassian, *Conferences*, edited by Boniface Ramsey, Ancient Christian Writers (Mahwah, NJ: Newman Press, 1997), 10.3.

anthropomorphism (or a more biblically based understanding of God) and Platonism. That is the luxury of the historian's hindsight – an account which in turn reflects the philosophical concerns of modernity.

Tradition can be seen looking forwards or backwards. Forwards, it is a matter of handing on a tradition. Naturally there will be a story to tell, a philosophical or theological narrative to express it, but what will be handed on is the practice of prayer, which is shaped by people's personal engagement with God. In relation to that, the framework used to support it is incidental and contingent. But looking back, tradition tends to be understood as the theological framework of the texts that record it. These have their own literary history, which will be narrated in response to whatever modern interests there are in it. However, at the heart of the process is a dynamic that engages a person's experience in faith, hope and love, where contextual issues are no more than that.

Dynamics of the tradition

Understanding the dynamics of this tradition is what patristic theology is about. It is concerned not only with the ideas and the theology of the Fathers of the Church, but also with the means and the methods by which theological ideas were developed and communicated in the available literature, as well as with the practices that support these texts. They bear witness to how Christians lived and learned their faith, how they found meaning for their lives and expressed it. The interest of Patristics in the way this literature reflects practice is similar to what Chapter 1 called a performative approach to contemplative awareness and prayer.

Many of these texts are liturgical, or commentaries on the Bible, but some of them are personal testimonies such as letters or private journals. As far as the contemplative tradition is concerned, three aspects seem to be particularly significant: the shape and form of liturgical worship, which involves architecture and art as well as ritual or cult; ways of reading the Bible; and the way we model ourselves on teachers, seek guidance from spiritual fathers and mothers and aspire to the example of saints and charismatic figures, as evidenced, for example, in martyrological texts, lives of saints and similar material. In their various ways, then, these texts witness to and nourished the faith and prayer of the early Church.

It is worth saying something at once about the way in which the Bible was read, since it is in connection to this that the actual term 'contemplation' in its Christian sense has its proper home. As will be seen, it is important to reconnect contemplative prayer with the Bible and its place in Christian life and worship. The Bible, understood as the Word of God, was seen as the foundation for the knowledge of God and for Christian teaching. It is wrong, then, to separate contemplation, even in the sense of contemplative prayer, from the ways in which Christians believe they learn to listen to the Word of God in the Bible. The Word of God was heard in this way above all in the liturgical worship of the Christian community, but also in the continual reading of it in private; and in doing so Christians were drawn to pay attention to the relationship reading brought about between God, the Church as a whole and the individual believer, a relationship in which Jesus Christ was believed to make himself present in the gift of the Holy Spirit.

All this is implicit in the way in which the Bible was commented on in liturgical homilies, as well as in commentaries written for personal study and teaching. It is implicit too in *lectio divina*.[6] The monastic practices of *lectio divina* were classically expressed by Guigo II, Prior of the Grande Chartreuse (1174–80; died c.1190), as the four steps of reading, meditation, prayer and contemplation.[7] They were closely modelled on the principles of exegesis used in preaching and in Christian teaching generally before the development of scholasticism. The evolution of monastic *lectio divina* out of classical methods of learning shows the development of a more affective and personal understanding of prayer as a way of cultivating a deeper knowledge of God.[8] Reading fed a personal appropriation of the sources of Christian wisdom; understood as taking place within a loving relationship with God, meditation and contemplation went beyond the academic dimension of learning. It is where

---

[6]On the developing tradition of *lectio divina*, see Raymond Studzinski, OSB, *Reading to Live: The Evolving Practice of 'Lectio Divina'* (Collegeville, MN: Liturgical Press, 2009); Duncan Robertson, *Lectio Divina: The Mediaeval Experience of Reading* (Collegeville, MN: Liturgical Press, 2011).
[7]Guigo II, *Ladder of Monks and Twelve Meditations*, edited by Edmund College and James Walsh (Kalamazoo, MI: Cistercian Publications, 1981).
[8]Pierre Hadot, *Philosophy as a Way of Life* (Oxford: Blackwell, 1995), and also his *Exercices spirituels et philosophie antique*, new edn (Paris: Albin Michel, 2002).

the question of a more personal understanding of experience arose within the dynamics of a contemplative tradition.

Later on, contemplation began to be dissociated from reading and meditation. It can be seen already in the English mystics and in texts like the anonymous *Cloud of Unknowing*, so that, by the seventeenth century, the question was when you should stop meditating in order to contemplate! But the earlier history illustrates what I mean by the dynamic of tradition. It shows how personal engagement with the tradition, in this case, through reading and writing, was pursued for its transformative effect thanks to the promotion of a contemplative experience of faith. Less needs to be said here as regards the liturgy, except to observe that *lectio divina*, and so contemplative prayer, was based on literature whose natural home was in worship, and that the liturgy was, especially for monks and nuns, what shaped their experience most of all. The third literary form supporting the context of contemplative prayer, lives and sayings, would have informed the transformative purpose of such meditative and contemplative practice, giving practical wisdom and examples to imitate.

Monks and nuns are a specialized group of people. But they are ordinary men and women, for the most part a silent witness to the dynamic of a contemplative tradition. When I think about the literature that communicated that tradition to them, and especially when I think about how it would have been received and used by them, I get a clear sense that, however important the contextual elements are in the tradition, what brings it to life is a personal engagement with God, which must have been, for them, the point of it all. Concepts like experience and subjectivity are complete anachronisms. No doubt they would have been simply mystified by them. However, it does not follow that they cannot be used in thinking about what they were trying to live, what gave ultimate meaning to their lives.

Modern mysticism and apophaticism

Modern mysticism is a label that has been given recently by a few studies of contemplative prayer and mystical theology that have noted how the terms 'mysticism' and *theologia mystica* came into circulation only in the late sixteenth and early seventeenth centuries. At that point, the idea of the 'mystical' was first used in relation to personal experience rather than to the meaning of scripture or to the sacraments. In the earlier tradition, 'mystical' refers not to specialized ways of knowing God, but to the Christian meaning of faith and practice, especially in terms of the Church's relationship to Jesus Christ. The change of reference in the seventeenth century is taken as evidence of the concerns at that time about epistemology and the 'subjective turn' associated with Descartes. It marks a shift towards the psychological dimension, which later on William James made the object of his studies. 'Modern mysticism', therefore, is used derogatively to refer to this shift of interest.

The apophatic tradition is an important aspect of this point of view, represented especially by Pseudo-Dionysius and Thomas

Gallus. Apophaticism is read by modern commentators as a critique of 'modern mysticism', especially of its alleged tendency to go off in the wrong direction, and to be distracted by the immediate psychological effects of prayer. As Denys Turner puts it in his *The Darkness of God*, mysticism, as opposed to 'modern mysticism', could be better described as anti-mysticism.[9] Peter Tyler follows the approach in his more recent work on Wittgenstein and Teresa of Avila.[10]

These commentators therefore see apophatic language as playing an ultimately rhetorical function, to subvert the reader from supposing that mystical theology is making substantive assertions about God. In Turner's mind, apophatic language not only negates affirmative theological statements about God; it has a more important second-order function too, to negate the opposition of the two terms. So, not only is God's being affirmed (the superlative use of affirmative discourse) but the terms of the affirmation are also negated; and, finally, the opposition of his being and non-being is denied. The logic of apophatic discourse is certainly paradoxical. The problem with this account is that the approach lends itself to a further and more sceptical view of God's unknowability, so that it denies the possibility not only of talking about him, but even of referring to him or of conceiving of his existence. That is to say, in the jargon of the modern philosophy of

---

[9]Denys Turner, *Darkness of God: Negativity in Christian Mysticism* (Cambridge: Cambridge University Press, 1998).
[10]Peter Tyler, *The Return to the Mystical: Ludwig Wittgenstein, Teresa of Avila and the Christian Mystical Tradition* (London: Continuum, 2011).

religion, it is an approach that is close to anti-realism, and to a number of postmodern philosophers.

This approach belongs to what has been called the performative reading of mysticism. But the interpretation of apophatic discourse in terms of a grammatical function gives it a different twist from the way it is presented by Sells. Turner's interest in apophaticism is less about how we promote the patterns of life that support contemplative experience than a critique of how some people might think we can.[11] The sceptical undertow of this approach comes through in some accounts more than in others. Whereas Sells argues that the paradoxical character of apophatic language sustains or holds a person in an 'anarchic meaning event' which, though expressed by 'unsaying', is a kind of knowing, Turner does not seem to be able to say this at all. Turner is suspicious, not of an unhealthy interest in experience, but rather of experience as such. His interpretation suggests that language collapses, and the resulting silence is empty in a very different way.[12]

It is certainly an effective riposte to William James and 'modern mysticism'. But it seems to throw the baby out with the bath water. It is another example of how a contemporary interest in mysticism is focused on other concerns than on understanding the contemplative experience of people who actually pray.

---

[11]Bernard McGinn reviews Turner's book in *Journal of Religion* 77 (1997), 309–11.
[12]See Louise Nelstrop, *Christian Mysticism*, pp. 57–8.

A corollary of this discussion is that, for all the changes in social practice and language that belong to the context of contemplative life in the seventeenth century, there is little to support an argument that what contemplatives were trying to do had changed from the earlier tradition. Certainly the language indicates a new concern with experience and especially personal experience, but that does not necessarily mean that people were being beguiled by the errors of 'modern mysticism'. The epistemological issues, complicated by the tormented story of the theology of grace, promoted a literature about stages of prayer and progress, and exposed deep anxieties about boundaries between ordinary levels of prayer and mystical states, and about the interplay between activity and passivity. Whether this was for better or worse is a question for scholars to evaluate. But the hindsight and perspectives deployed in doing so cannot controvert what to my mind is a complex but continuous tradition of praying, where people were seeking for God and, in various ways, finding him.

Shape of the traditional framework

Here I will attempt only a general overview of the traditional picture, in order to delineate the major structural elements, before highlighting the points, from a philosophical perspective, where the joints would probably be felt to be less secure.

Perhaps the most obvious element of this framework is the idea of a fundamental shift in prayer from the visible to the invisible, from the material to the spiritual, from the sensible to the intellectual. The underlying model is one where the mind, suitably purified and equipped, has immediate access to the world of Forms. The Forms are the rational basis of everything's being what it is, and it is expressed most vividly in the analogies of the Sun and the Cave in Plato's *Republic*. The model ensures an understanding of knowledge that is non-discursive and contemplative, where the intellect transcends the operation of propositional reasoning.

Christian versions of this model, where the Forms are closely related to the mind of God, emphasize that it is not only about intellectual knowledge of God. It is a matter of desire, and the need for conversion affects the transformation of the entire human being and human feeling. The affective dimension in prayer became more prominent in the monastic tradition; the Pauline opposition of faith and knowledge (especially in the later scholastic context) gave a clearer and more prominent role to the human will. But, in general, feelings were not important; they were misleading and could even be dangerous. More important was a deeper kind of desiring. Intellectual desire was *different*.

A compelling idea in all this is the notion of the Absolute. The contingencies of life, besides the question posed by the startling fact of existence, easily seemed to call for unconditional being to serve as a necessary basis for being (able to be) sure about things. In so far as a rational account was needed for belief in God's existence, it was generally grounded in this kind of way, notably articulated in the famous radio discussion in 1948 between Bertrand Russell and Fr Frederick Copleston. The argument from design used to have an obviousness too, for all the counter-evidence, like the notorious 1755 Lisbon earthquake, cited on the other side of the argument. The moral dimension of life, the claim of conscience and the sheer sense of obligation were another way to open up, as in Kant, the question of the experience of God.

Implicit in this kind of account are three structural elements. First, there is the idea of the mind's connaturality with the source of reality, and the ultimately intellectual character of that. Human beings as intellectual creatures occupy a middle position between the natural and the supernatural, the material and the spiritual, and this dual schema (while not necessarily dualism in a bad sense) runs through their mental and moral life. But human nature has a fundamentally spiritual vocation that is fully realized in contemplation, if not in this life, then in the life to come.

That is not to deny the part that the incarnation and redemption play. Grace and the work of transformation are the way in which the very non-Platonic issues of sin and death are addressed. Augustine's comparison between Platonism and the Gospel based on the Prologue of St John's Gospel is a famous reflection on the inadequacy of intellect alone.[13] But, although the Scotist Franciscan tradition saw the problem, the general

---

[13] Augustine, *Confessions*, edited by Maria Boulding and John E. Rotelle (Hyde Park, NY: New City Press, 1997), VII.ix.13.

view was that the incarnation was motivated by the need for redemption; it is easy to get the impression that this was rather what has come to be called a Plan B.

The second element is the place God or the Absolute takes in this. He is understood as the foundation to the existence of everything. This prompts the argument that God is therefore not part of that reality; but the relation between God and reality, however it is understood, has a rational structure that makes possible a natural theology. Accordingly, the world is a mirror that reflects the divine reality. In itself, the divine reality is beyond our ability to see and reflect on, but we can move towards knowledge of God on the basis of the things he has created and which reflect his glory and his purpose.

Third, the mind's ability intellectually to grasp truth and to understand its divine meaning is thanks to its being illuminated by God. Augustine's narrative in his *Confessions* of his visions, at Milan and at Ostia, makes an important contribution to this.[14] Theories of analogy were developed to express how created reality can express divine meaning. This is the context for a proper appreciation of apophaticism, which aims to preserve the gap between the possibilities for understanding divine meaning in the created order and God's own transcendence of that meaning in himself.

While an analogy had been drawn between the sacramental sense of the mystical journey and the personal life of prayer, the influence of Pseudo-Dionysius on contemplative writing

---

[14]Augustine, *Confessions*, VII.x.16–xvii.23; IX.x.23–5; X.xxvii.38.

contributed to the description of a further stage in which deeper spiritual work was understood as being done largely in darkness by (and for) the soul that is seeking union with God. In contrast to the reading of apophaticism by some modern performative theorists, the traditional understanding deploys notions, of both light and of dark, in a non-exclusive way: it is an obscure light ('in a mirror, darkly'[15]) or it is a radiant darkness.

Such a brief synthesis will seem cavalier only if the point of attempting it is forgotten. That was to articulate some of the main elements that, generally speaking, have been implicit in the framework used to tell the story of the contemplative tradition in traditional terms. It is, I should say, a framework that still underlies books on contemplative prayer, and which is implicit in much Christian spiritual discourse. At the risk of oversimplification, though, I wanted to highlight some of the features of the three philosophical domains of epistemology, metaphysics, and meaning and language where traditional ideas no longer have the obviousness they used to for people who are strangers to the tradition.

Difficulties with accessing the tradition today

Perhaps the most problematic of the challenges that has been raised against this tradition is what goes by the name

---

[15] 1 Corinthians 13.12 (ERV).

of dualism. The prominence of binomial schemes, like mind/body, interior/exterior, natural/supernatural, has led to the charge of opposing the visible and material world to an invisible, spiritual one. This is less than just to Plato and, in spite of some Christian tendencies to the contrary, the Christian tradition has not by and large understood these logical distinctions as disparaging one term against the other. The problem is that the attribution of higher ontological value to one rather than the other, of its being 'more real' than the other, has lost its plausibility with the disappearance of a vertical conception of structure to reality in terms of greater and less being. While the binomial used to be a way of thinking about relationship as well as contrast, there is no longer a way of conceiving that kind of ontological relationship in terms of a supposedly higher level of being in some sense containing or embracing a lower one or one in relation to which opposites can be reconciled. To see the contemplative life as involving some kind of move from one to the other exposes this problem rather sharply.

The question of mind/body dualism in Descartes is different. In some circles, Cartesianism has become a terrible slur. It is clear that Descartes was compelled to insist on an opposition of the mind, understood in a specific way, and the body because he needed to establish a person's ability to be certain, so as to establish the grounds for a person's own knowledge and understanding, rather than simply relying on somebody else's word for it. To be sure, Descartes had reasons for trying to find a new way of establishing knowledge independently of the authority of institutions or authority figures, but it is also clear that intellectual activity takes place in a tradition that cannot be occluded so straightforwardly; in the end, the solitary individual, sure of his or her own subjectivity and of standing epistemically apart from an object of detached knowledge, is a myth, which has had huge consequences in the European cultural tradition.

The modern outlook has been deeply influenced by Descartes in its interest in subjectivity and the isolation of the epistemic subject, and this has compromised the way we access the earlier tradition. These ideas have affected the contemplative tradition too. Descartes' emphasis on the individual 'knower', and on interiority *in opposition to* exteriority, distorts older Augustinian perspectives. It isolates the person at prayer from communal contexts of worship. A corollary too is that the Cartesian separation of mind and body compromises the emotional dimension of spiritual intelligence. Descartes does acknowledge the emotions, and he does not dissociate a person's mind and body as if they were alien to each other. But the scope of the affective dimension of experience or the dynamics of intersubjectivity, both of which have been given a higher profile in recent thinking about knowledge, do not receive the attention they deserve. On the contrary, the strong emphasis on interiority tends to isolate the search for God from wider contexts of meaning. Descartes' idea that God was introspectively knowable (a form of the ontological argument), and that his being was taken to be metaphysically necessary, also contribute to what is ultimately a fundamentally different notion of our relationship to God from the patristic tradition.[16]

Another area of serious difficulty, this time with the early tradition itself, is over the ontological relationship between God and the metaphysical notion of the being of reality. The difficulty is over what seems to be a simplification of the notion of being in later scholasticism. Plato talked about reality in all sorts of ways, distinguishing the relative nature of the world of change from the true reality of the intelligible principles or Forms that underlie it. He distinguishes those from the ultimate principle, the Form of Good, whose sheer perfection puts it 'beyond being'. Aristotle was more interested in the fact that things come to be, and in the kinds of explanation that invites. But, at the same time, being becomes more a fact in its own right, and as such it acquires a kind of uniform status as a truth. Things are all sorts of things in all sorts of ways, but the fact that they are is pretty much a single kind of thing. Being can come to be seen as something everything shares, and which God shares in a supreme way. Aquinas was under no illusions about God's difference from what he brings into being. He had a rigorous sense of divine simplicity, of the impossibility of introducing distinctions into our thinking about God that we cannot but use in thinking about anything else. But it is not a big step from seeing God's sheer existence as *creator* as

---

[16]The impact is seen in the thinking of the early English Benedictine monk, Dom Augustine Baker. On this, see John Cottingham, 'The spiritual and the philosophical quest: Augustine Baker and René Descartes', in Geoffrey Scott (ed.), *Dom Augustine Baker 1575–1641* (Leominster: Gracewing, 2012) pp. 153–78.

the fundamental reason that something rather than nothing exists, even though it is accepted that his nature is beyond our understanding, to thinking that God is the *foundation* of reality, and that this foundation is provided by his nature as supreme, absolute, necessary being.

So the problem that arises for a contemporary appreciation of the contemplative tradition is twofold. On the one hand, the alignment of this kind of foundational being with God makes for a very different God from the personal God of compassionate love and beauty revealed in Jesus Christ, who is sought in faith, hope and love. On the other hand, the metaphysical objections to such a kind of being, enunciated initially by Kant as 'onto-theology' – a term taken up by Heidegger as a diagnosis of the problem of the European metaphysical tradition as a whole – mean that the contemplative tradition is compromised, too, in its classic forms of expression.

Finally, there is a group of concerns that bear on meaning and affectivity. Essential to the contemplative tradition is the understanding of *intellectus* as a non-conceptual grasp of reality. The close links in the Platonic tradition between truth and beauty, for example in Plato's *Symposium* or *Phaedrus*, are important. They allow for the possibility of engaging with reality even when it goes beyond our ability to put things into words. Affectivity comes in here. The truth can be loved even when it exceeds our minds. Indeed love draws the mind to further insight. In such a picture of reality, knowledge can be understood in personal terms, and the ultimate truth can be presented in terms of a relationship in which a person grows in virtue and even finds life. The relationship between the human being and God is nurtured especially by the way that God makes his presence and intentions felt in the world of experience through which we are drawn to enjoy the source of being, meaning and value.

The shifts in later scholasticism over the understanding of being went with the wider impact of nominalism, which shattered the relationships of meaning between God and the created order. Meaning became a matter of human conventions of naming. This had colossal consequences for our ability to understand contemplative life. *Intellectus* lost its affinity to a personal relationship of love with the ultimate source of meaning. In its place came an emphasis on the role of the (blind) will as our means of adhesion to God to try to make up the loss. It is no surprise to find a reinforced stress on the ideas of will and obedience, with all the inhibitions that ensue for what had been regarded as a natural inclination to the search for God. The human being has to become passive to the grace of a God whose thoughts are not our thoughts; while, conversely, recognizing that passivity is scarcely an adequate response to the initiative of divine grace. Perhaps it is no surprise that, in the theological travails in Roman Catholicism of the seventeenth to twentieth centuries, the contemplative life suffered.

Wonder became an intellectual puzzle for science, not for prayer. Romanticism certainly responded to a sense of transcendent mystery revealed in the new worlds that were opening up aesthetically, and which evoked a sense of the beyond; but, after Kant, this was *beyond the phenomena*. It was unknowable. The resonances in Romantic literature with Augustine are clear, and the aesthetic dimension that is engaged speaks again to contemplative awareness; but the resonances are, in contrast to Augustine's strongly incarnational theology, and to the centrality of Jesus in his thinking, disembodied sounds stirring 'intimations of immortality' (to use Wordsworth's phrase), but not redeeming or transforming the soul.

Conclusion

In the last two sections I have hazarded an outline in rather broad terms of three kinds of problem where the development of the philosophical tradition, from later scholasticism and through the period since Descartes, has had ramifications on the classic contemplative tradition. To some extent, the tradition has compromised the proper understanding of that tradition by people who pray; to some extent, it has made it less accessible to people who are unfamiliar with it, or who are sceptical about its philosophical commitments. I have also argued that some responses to modern philosophical interests that have sought to refer to and to renew interest in earlier thinking about mysticism especially are misleading, both as interpretations of the earlier tradition and as a contribution to any renewal of understanding of contemplative prayer as it is actually practised.

At the same time, I do believe there is a traditional practice of contemplative prayer, which has been communicated within all the complexities of theological explanation and philosophical styles of understanding, as well as in spite of the challenges it has faced by being misrepresented or misunderstood.

This chapter has focused on three areas of concern over the framework used to support the practice of contemplative prayer. They are about human subjectivity and knowledge, our understanding of God in relation to being, and the relation of meaning and affectivity. Here I think a different approach might help in the construction of a new framework for understanding it.

Appendix

Interpretation of Pseudo-Dionysius and performative mysticism

Apophaticism and Pseudo-Dionysius play an important part in any account of Christian mysticism and of contemplative prayer, but a particular question arises over the way in which commentators like Denys Turner understand the function of *apophasis* in what has been called a performative interpretation of mysticism. I want to consider the relevant text more closely here.[17]

---

[17]I refer to the Greek of Pseudo-Dionysius' *Mystical Theology* by the Migne PG numbers. The critical edition is Pseudo-Dionysius Areopagita, *De Coelesti Hierarchia, De Ecclesiastica Hierarchia, De Mystica Theologia, Epistulae*, Corpus Dionysiacum Band 2, Patristische Texte und Studien 36, edited by Günter Heil and Adolf M. Ritter (Berlin: Walter de Gruyter, 1991); English translation in Pseudo-Dionysius, *The Complete Works*, Classics of Western Spirituality, translated by Colm Luibhéid and Paul Rorem (New York: Paulist Press, 1987).

The opening words of the *Mystical Theology* show that the rhetorical cast of the text is to be read (performatively) in terms of prayer (and liturgy). In so far as it makes extensive use of technical language, it does not set out to be a logical or epistemological discourse, and the poetic sensibility of hymnody (1025A) is also needed.

In the first chapter he speaks of the luminous cloud of silence that teaches in a hidden way and fills the unseeing understanding with resplendent marvels, which are completely insensible and invisible. So Timothy is urged to reach out to union (*henosis*) beyond sense perception and intellectual concepts in an act of unknowing (*agnosis*). The author speaks of ecstasy – reaching out (an Italian translation catches the sense of 'tension') beyond the self and everything, raised up by God (997B–1000A). The question is how this is to be done and, in particular, the way in which the reaching out beyond everything relates to the performative use of language.

A crucial paragraph follows.[18] God is transcendent (supersubstantial) and known without words or concepts. We need to be affirmative (*kataphaskein theseis*) and to be negative, denying the affirmations (*apophaskein autas*). This is said to be *kurioteron* – more important, but the root word in Greek suggests the implied reason that it is more fundamental, more secure (1000B). For, in so far as God exceeds everything, we must not assume that a denial (*apophasis*) is opposite to the

---

[18]I am grateful to Andrew Louth for drawing attention to this in a private conversation in December 2011.

assertion (*kataphasis*), but much more that the Godhead stands above all (assertions of) lack (*stereseis*) as being beyond any negation (lit. taking away, *aphairesis*) and assertion (lit. putting, *thesis*). Such an idea of lack, or shortfall, could be suggested by the limitations implicit in the attribution of any finite term to God, as well as in the denial of it.

Against this reading of the Greek, Turner seems to assume that *steresis* is the same as *apophasis*, and to refer to the act of taking away or denial, rather than to the property (or lack of it) that might be asserted or denied. This is the second move of negation that is crucial for Turner's denial of the opposition between all positives and negatives. For Turner, God is simply beyond. Our union with him is left without any rational framework, in a beyond-being that is contrary to any understanding of being. But I am suggesting that *steresis* is to be understood differently.

The end of the first chapter is also important (1001A). Moses is the analogue for the mystic. He is described as entering the cloud of unknowing (*agnosia*), as wholly belonging to the one that is beyond everything and nothing, and not to himself nor to anything else, being united as far as possible by an inoperativeness of all knowledge (*tei pases gnoseos anergesiai*) to the one that is utterly unknowable (*toi pantelos agnostoi*) and knowing him (*gignoskon*) beyond the intellect (*hyper noun*) by a failure of knowledge (*toi meden ginoskein*).

The intellectualist cast of this is clear, and for all the apophaticism the final word in the Greek is the positive verb for 'knowing', clearly an important point for appreciating the line of Dionysius' argument. The question is how knowing is done in relation to God, given the uniqueness of God's relation to everything else as well as in himself. Dionysius talks of 'inoperativeness' of knowledge, joining the negative prefix *an-* to the idea of 'working'. The standard translation is 'inactivity', which suggests simply refraining from thinking. But this would fail to capture the more complex processes earlier described, and which are recapitulated in the observation that Moses kept quiet from uttering all cognitive conceptions (*apomuei pasas tas gnostikas antilepseis*). The idea of inoperativeness suggests the frustration of all positive and negative cognitive processes, which reduce a person to silence; it does not mean passivity or inertia, but a state of cognitive tension. This tension is the *ekstasis* of unknowing; in fact, the Greek verb *apomuein* might prompt a translation like Sells' term, 'to unsay'.

The issue here is that there are two possible interpretations of the apophatic. In one, God is beyond language, and the paradoxes and oxymorons show how language breaks down, forcing a soul to find contact with God in some mysterious way beyond the cognitive and conceptual field of experience. I guess this may be the common reading of mysticism, in which a person moves ecstatically into a new and higher plane of being, where union with God takes place. The other interpretation is less exciting perhaps, but probably more intelligible, however mysterious it naturally remains. In this reading of Dionysius, God is known in the very conflict of language, and in the frustration of any attempt to put divine truth into words. The knowing is distinctive; the unknowing functions in relation to the peculiar logic that requires us to talk in oxymorons and paradox. The *ekstasis* lies in the way the semantic tensions draw us into a different kind of awareness, in which God (who is beyond any of the limitations that are implicit in finite concepts) nevertheless makes his presence felt.[19]

---

[19]Massimiliano Zupi discusses this in his study of Platonism in the mysticism of Gregory of Nyssa, *Incanto e incantesimo dire*, Studia Anselmiana 143 (Rome: Sant'Anselmo, 2007), especially pp. 684–6.

3

New Starting Points

The problems that have been found in the traditional framework of contemplative prayer are a matter of theory, and those who actually pray will rightly regard them as merely theoretical issues. But I am concerned that prayer has become detached from philosophical culture. This has two consequences independent of religious faith: first, the appreciation of contemplative experience as such is lost, as well as the disciplines needed to promote and persevere in it; second, that people interested in philosophy misconstrue contemplative practice. The result is that the contribution that contemplative experience can make to the contemporary world, with or without Christian faith, is overlooked.

Putting the point controversially, the problems of contemporary culture that Nietzsche memorably noted as the 'death of God', which plays into so many of the serious difficulties of contemporary society, calls for contemplatives rather than for postmodern relativism and scepticism. Even though the cultural analysis given by postmodernism often spells out the issues most clearly, I think they need to be addressed on the basis of the renewal of the depth of human awareness that the contemplative tradition promoted in the past.

That is why, in the attempt to find new starting points for understanding contemplative prayer, I think it is doubly important to work with people like Nietzsche and Heidegger. On the one hand, they articulate the human predicament in a way that exposes the human problem, to which prayer is also a response, but with which it also has to struggle. On the other, their influence on the contemporary situation and on philosophical responses to it is so strong that someone who is concerned with the role of contemplative prayer in modern life must necessarily work in dialogue with them.

Nihilism

The label of nihilism has been stuck onto several things. This chapter will focus above all on Friedrich Nietzsche (1844–1900) and on Martin Heidegger (1889–1976). The story goes back to before them. Philosophically, 'nihilism' was used as a term by Friedrich Jacobi (1743–1819), who criticized the idealism he saw in Kantian philosophy; that is to say, if a person could have no knowledge of something as it is in itself, and if our knowledge depended fundamentally on our own mental structures (categories), we could not say that reality existed independently of our knowledge of it. This was what he meant by nihilism.

Immanuel Kant (1724–1804) certainly believed in the external and independent reality of the objects of our knowledge, and (not unlike Jacobi) he hoped to delimit overweening claims to knowledge in order, as he said, to allow proper scope for faith.[1] But his insight into the constructive way the human mind engages with the external world could lead, as in 'idealists' like J. G. Fichte (1762–1814), F. W. J. von Schelling (1775–1854) or G. W. F. Hegel (1770–1831), to the idea that the world was in some way constructed by the human mind. The crux was that this identified the conditions for knowing something with the conditions for the existence of something, because there was no further way of knowing that, or of distinguishing between the world as it is in itself and the world that we know in the (consequently constructive) ways that we did. Nietzsche is a radical exponent of such an approach in the way he develops his criticism of the constructive interest we take in how we see things and say how they are.

The broader background to nihilism is relevant. It queries the pretensions of rationality and explores the dimension of faith. Søren Kierkegaard (1813–55), in marked reaction to the ambitions of Hegelian *Geist* (mind or spirit), focused attention on the human sense of meaninglessness, which resulted from suppressing a person's sense of individuality, a malaise he called 'levelling'. The source of alienation was the human being's inability to make the commitments entailed in the responsibility a person has for living a life. This meant going

---

[1]Immanuel Kant, *Critique of Pure Reason*, edited by Paul Guyer and Allen W. Wood (Cambridge: Cambridge University Press, 1998), B xxx.

beyond rational categories of utility and even ethics towards the religious; even if it was not specifically articulated in these terms, the existential commitment needed was analogous to it, not based on standard rationality. In the face of the decisiveness of such commitments, for which a person stands under an eternal judgement, experience is paralysed by the tension between anxiety (*Angst*) and freedom. George Brandes, a Danish philosopher, who recommended Kierkegaard's work to Nietzsche in 1888, saw the potential interest of these ideas to Nietzsche.[2] But his 1889 illness prevented him from doing anything about them.

Ivan Turgenev's novel *Fathers and Sons* (1862) gave the term 'nihilist' a social and political currency, and it came to be used to refer to the insurrectionists who assassinated Tsar Alexander II in 1881, and to similar radical and violent movements at the end of the nineteenth century. Fyodor Dostoevsky (1821–81), while no nihilist in that sense, was interested in what went on in the margins of Russian social life and in the experience of what he calls the 'underground man'. This had an impact on Nietzsche, who recognized Dostoevsky's insight into human character.[3] The 'underground man', detached from the norms and reasoning of cultivated society, and therefore a man as sceptical of the interests at work in conventional rationality as Nietzsche, is a person for whom the violence of human

[2]Malcolm Brown, *Nietzsche Chronicle*, www.dartmouth.edu/~fnchron/1888.html (accessed 12 November 2014).
[3]Friedrich Nietzsche, Letter to Peter Gast, 7 March 1887, www.thenietzschechannel. com/correspondence/eng/nlett-1887.htm (accessed 12 November 2014).

passion and the rawness of life are unveiled. The question of the meaning or meaninglessness of the margin (or underside) of life is a continual question. Dostoevsky's paradoxical contrast between Christ and the truth – and his preference for Christ – is a reminder that in this area of experience rationality is at work in a different kind of way.[4]

Nietzsche is not a lone figure, then, in relation to nihilism, either in the philosophical sense or in his appreciation of the human malaise. This was a sense of loss of meaning and disorientation, as well as of the irrational and paradoxical elements in human life, which challenged the social, political and philosophical conventions of the day. Nietzsche's awareness of it, and his attempt to understand what it meant and to respond to it are what made his thinking compelling to people like Heidegger in the dislocations of Nazi Germany and the development of technological modernity, and in postmodernism.

Nietzsche

Nietzsche offered a response to this problem, and wanted to show that there was a way out of the malaise. It called for a diagnosis of what he saw as inherent in the European tradition of philosophy. He accepted, then, the Jacobi-kind

---

[4]Rowan Williams, *Dostoevsky: Language, Faith and Fiction* (London: Continuum, 2008) is a good study of the ramifications of this.

of critique of Kantianism. But he also argued that the process was inevitable and a necessary stage on the way to realizing the truth about life. It was important to acknowledge it and not to see oneself as the victim of something about which there was nothing to be done. That people felt bad in their situation, alienated and anxious, was the result of a systematic mistake, a deception, even, which was the cause of the disease. This was the Judaeo-Christian tradition that Nietzsche saw lying at the foundation of the European philosophical tradition. He believed that the problem lay in its metaphysics, which were grounded on an idea of God, Platonic before it was Christian, as ultimate being. He argued that the tradition was designed to make people feel bad, because the values it enshrined were false.

The way out of the difficulty called not for a change of mind, but a change of heart. The world-denying values of Christianity suppressed the real energy of life. Nietzsche contrasted the Dionysian power of creativity with the rationalism of Apollo. The cure required a therapeutic process of recovery, beginning with waking up to the truth and then systematically disabusing oneself of the habits of error. Health depended on the 'transvaluation of value' and a transvaluation of the current human condition by an assertion of the sheer power of life, as opposed to doing obeisance to the power of God or any of his many substitutes. The realization of human life 'beyond' is called the 'overman' (*Übermensch*). He is the person who 'goes over'; the traditional translation of 'Superman' (that is, 'stands over') is a misleading caricature. Nietzsche called it the Will to Power, the title of the collection of notebooks that his sister published after his death.

Nihilism has two senses in Nietzsche, bad as well as good, depending on whether it refers to the malaise or the cure. And he thinks that some responses to the problem, like Christianity, are also pathological; they only reinforce the symptoms of the disease. But atheism can be pathological too. Schopenhauer is criticized for his fundamental pessimism towards life; his interest in the arts and in creating meaning is an attempt to escape from the truth about life, a refusal of the rapture of it. His interest in Buddhism is another sign of its denial.

Ironically, Arthur Schopenhauer (1788–1860) had already recognized the possibility that the human will might be a way of addressing the philosophical problem central to Kant's philosophy, how we could know (when we only have the 'phenomenon' to go by) that there is a reality beyond the subjectivity of our perception. Schopenhauer recognized that there were other dimensions to our engagement with things as a whole than rationality; and in art and creativity, in sex as well as in our unconscious, we are engaged in things more than just as knowers of it. He referred to this non-cognitive participation in reality as 'Will' (the German meaning more than the English word), which became Nietzsche's keyword. For Nietzsche, will is something that needs to be asserted, not just part of the way things are and in which we participate. Passivity like that is another symptom of the pathology.

Denying the real dynamism of life is the critical error.
It was, above all, the problem with the asceticism of the
Christian tradition. The moral and religious tradition, with
the metaphysics that went with it, reinforced it. In contrast to
Kierkegaard, human life had not suffered a loss of meaning
and direction; Nietzsche argued that we have to win our
way through to it. No other authority could give it to us. So
nihilism, in its good sense, lies in the recognition that we
cannot owe our salvation to anyone else. We have to take life as
it is and make it what it needs to be.

Giles Fraser, in his *Redeeming Nietzsche*, highlights the
structure of pathology, diagnosis and cure in this thinking,
and develops it in terms of a model of redemption. In
contrast to a classic Platonic-Augustinian model, Nietzsche
proposes a radical alternative.[5] In fact, he proposes two:
an earlier one, influenced by Schopenhauer, in terms of
art; a later one developed in dialectic with his critique of
Christianity, in the direction of the *Übermensch*. The earlier
is found in *The Birth of Tragedy* (1872), in the period when
he still admired Wagner; the later is exemplified in the *On
the Genealogy of Morals* (1887) and *The Anti-Christ* (1888).
Fraser argues that Nietzsche makes some telling challenges to
a Christian soteriology, including the dangers of self-hatred
or *ressentiment*, self-pity and the victim mentality, the whole
way in which trying to talk about a 'better world' leads to

[5]Giles Fraser, *Redeeming Nietzsche: On the Piety of Unbelief* (London: Routledge, 2002), p. 49.

avoiding truth, avoiding acknowledgement of the tragic dimension of life; but, against that, the fundamental weakness in a Nietzschean remedy for the human predicament is that it greatly underestimates the horror of the situation, which undermines any effort of human beings to will their way to a transformation of human being and society.

Death of God

Nietzsche was sure that his time was a critical moment for philosophy. The parable of the death of God in *The Gay Science* (1882) puts the issue succinctly.[6] Far from celebrating the vindication of atheism, the madman is looking for God; and his audience, largely already atheist, make fun of him. His prophetic message is not that God has died, but that, as if unawares, they have all murdered him and fail to appreciate the full horror of what they have done. The world has become empty, dark and cold, unintelligible. The question is how they were able to drink up the sea and sponge away the horizon. How were they able to erase God from the world-view for which they are still nostalgic, in some sense still need?

Nihilism then speaks to a very ambivalent moment, far from being a simple moment of liberation; it is a time of profound disorientation. Nietzsche is aware how easy it is to

---

[6]Friedrich Nietzsche, *The Gay Science*, edited by Bernard Williams, Cambridge Texts in the History of Philosophy (Cambridge: Cambridge University Press, 2001), section 125.

shy away from the call to truth, and that we prefer to deceive ourselves, and to live out a spiritual fantasy, creating other false gods to serve (including the danger of nationalism).[7] He finds himself, then, in a lonely position, having come too early. A new philosophy is called for, but no one seems interested. Nonetheless, Nietzsche has good news, of new worlds to discover, of the fresh air of truthfulness where one can pursue beauty and desire. For all the critique of Christian morality and asceticism, he speaks in two sections of a new contemplative life, where people know how to improvise living (we should think, no doubt, of the Dionysian freedom of the jazz player), and above all know how to live tragedy out into redemption.[8] To use a phrase of Alex McIntyre, 'joy in the actual' is a powerful idea.[9]

Nietzsche raises a challenge to traditional metaphysics, especially in view of his argument that traditional metaphysics has, as it were, burnt itself out. We have grown out of the securities of a religiously explained world and cannot live in the same way again. We have to learn to live differently and, above all, without depending on God to be the foundation of everything. We have to learn to ground our intelligence of life on ourselves. There is everything to be gained by this, but we have to take our selves as they really are, and also to cultivate rigorous honesty, in a positive and not a negative light.

---

[7]Nietzsche, *Gay Science*, sections 319, 344, 347.
[8]Nietzsche, *Gay Science*, sections 289, 293, 299, 301, 303.
[9]Alex McIntyre, *Sovereignty of Joy: Nietzsche's Vision of Grand Politics* (Toronto: University of Toronto Press, 1997).

Heidegger as a reader of Nietzsche

Heidegger wrote a monograph in 1943 entitled 'Nietzsche's word: "God is dead"', published in *Off the Beaten Track* (*Holzwege*).[10] The importance of the parable was not lost on him. His interest in Nietzsche dates back to the years immediately following the publication in 1927 of *Being and Time*. The two volumes in the German *Collected Works* that carry Nietzsche's name include work that dates from 1930 and the lectures given between 1936 and 1946, the period, that is, after his resignation from the rectorship of Freiburg and through the Second World War.[11] Nietzsche (in folk imagination, a guru of the futurism projected by Nazism) was the companion of Heidegger's retirement from a Nazi revaluation of values and his disillusionment with that kind of *Übermensch*.

Heidegger's interest in Nietzsche prompted a reappraisal of Nietzsche's philosophical work. His interpretation is based on a critical reading of Nietzsche's metaphysics rather than his moral philosophy. According to Heidegger, the death of God is a recognition that the place that God had occupied in

---

[10]Martin Heidegger, *Off the Beaten Track*, edited and translated by Julian Young and Kenneth Haynes (Cambridge: Cambridge University Press, 2002), pp. 157–99. There is an excellent chronology of Heidegger's life in the Italian edition of *Being and Time*: Martin Heidegger, *Essere e tempo*, Edizione Italiana a Cura di Alfredo Marini con Testo Tedesco a Fronte, 3rd edn (Milan: Mondadori, 2013), pp. xliii–cxvi. This edition also contains a German–Italian index to a lexicon (of the Italian terminology used in the translation), and an exhaustive list of Heidegger's work.

[11]Martin Heidegger, *Gesamtausgabe*, 6:1 and 6:2; the English translation omits several pieces: *Nietzsche 1936–1953*, 4 vols, translated by David Farrell Krell (New York: Harper & Row, 1979–87).

metaphysics was no longer tenable. While Nietzsche had seen the movement of the European intellectual tradition to nihilism in moral terms, calling for a revaluation of values, Heidegger thought this diagnosis did not go far enough. Nietzsche was himself in thrall to Kant when he assumed that he could separate off value from the essence of things, and to Descartes' radical distinction of the subject and object, which was entailed by a revaluation of everything by a 'super-human' subject on the basis of the Will to Power. It was only a further twist in the nihilist disease.

For Heidegger, Nietzsche did not provide the key to resolving the human problem but he did make clear what the key was. If he was not the prophet of its redemption, Nietzsche had appreciated how thinking, for all its errors, is indebted to its tradition; that we are completely part of the story that has to be recovered in order to move on in better health. So, for Heidegger, the focus on the subjectivity of the person who wills the values is the error, and the recovery involves overcoming the opposition of subject and object that underlies the Will to Power.

Heidegger's path to recovery also called for a diagnostic understanding of the way the tradition had continually got it wrong. He therefore pursued a hermeneutic analysis of the tradition in order to recover the original insight about being as an insight into the error. On that basis, it would be possible to find a therapy, in Nietzsche's terms, a way of rethinking the intervening history towards a better way forwards. The word for this was *Überwindung*. The literal meaning is 'overcoming', but in contrast to Nietzsche, who saw the task very much as a reversal of erroneous thinking, Heidegger does not think about inflicting defeat on an opponent; 'surpassing' is about understanding what the formation and development of a tradition takes rather for granted; the implicit issues need to be made explicit in order to go beyond it.

Heidegger's reading of Nietzsche is a critical dialogue with him and contributes to the development of the primarily metaphysical, or ontological, concerns Heidegger had sought to unpack in *Being and Time*. As a response to nihilism, Heidegger returns more radically to the question of being, and in particular to the ways in which he believed that it is continually overlooked, or occluded, by other concerns. The true diagnosis for Heidegger of the human predicament was not the denial of life; it was the forgetfulness of being.[12]

Recovering the question of being

What went wrong with thinking about being? Heidegger notes how the difficulty of the question had been repeatedly avoided. The root problem was labelled 'onto-theology', although God

---

[12]For discussions of Heidegger I have found particularly useful, see: Hubert L. Dreyfus and Mark A. Wrathall (eds), *A Companion to Heidegger* (Oxford: Blackwell, 2005); Charles B. Guignon (ed.), *The Cambridge Companion to Heidegger*, 2nd edn (Cambridge: Cambridge University Press, 2006); John Richardson, *Heidegger* (Abingdon: Routledge, 2012); Mark A. Wrathall, *Heidegger and Unconcealment: Truth, Language and History* (Cambridge: Cambridge University Press, 2011).

is only one of the ways in which the problem manifested itself. 'Onto-theology' had been coined by Kant, in relation to his critique of pure reason, where he exposed the inadequacy of deductive arguments for the existence of God.[13] He discussed them in three categories: cosmo-theological (depending on a posteriori arguments, for example, of design), onto-theological (depending on a priori arguments, such as the ontological argument, of conceptual necessity) and teleological (based on purpose). For Kant, what lay beyond sense perception (the *noumenon*) was unknowable.

At any rate, in terms of pure reason, Kant had argued that there was no justification for grounding metaphysical explanations on God. But his own desire to justify faith in terms of practical reason, in his moral argument for God's existence, in fact used a different a priori argument. So, in the end, he too had an onto-theology, which operated in the field of practical reason. Heidegger's claim about the recalcitrance of onto-theology, even in the person who exposed it, could claim to be justified. God always ended up as the foundation of explanation. Kant's move to the idea of moral obligation was just further evidence of the pathology of our need for rational foundations. If God was not 'out there' in reality or in our consciences to sustain the structure, why bother? This is what, Jacobi argued, allowed for the possibility of nihilism. Nihilism arises when that foundation is no longer needed. God has passed away, and it is the philosopher who has been

---

[13]Kant, *Critique of Pure Reason*, A632/B660.

responsible. Heidegger would try to address the response to nihilism in a completely different way.

In *Being and Time*, Heidegger was concerned about the role God came to play in the metaphysical system, which he believed was inherent in the Western metaphysical tradition. This was where he sympathized with Nietzsche's diagnosis of the metaphysical problem. For Heidegger, the systematic mistake about being made by philosophy worked itself out in the way people resorted to God or equivalent notions. Heidegger wanted to 'surpass' the problem with a phenomenological recovery of the truth of being, seeking an exact account of how we actually experience it. God was too quick an answer to the 'how come?' question because it worked only by positing another being, about which the same kind of question arose.

The problem was not only with the concept of God, but also with any concept used to offer a fundamental level of explanation, where philosophers continually introduced into the explanation of the being of anything something that was itself proposed as fundamental but whose own being needed explanation. In the meantime, what being was in itself was overlooked. It was the same problem with the use of Forms in Plato, or act in Aristotle; in Kant it took a transcendental turn, so that human subjectivity became the foundation for certainty; will played analogous roles in Schopenhauer or Nietzsche. And, as Heidegger's later philosophy showed, the same problem arose in the modern world, where technology had taken over from metaphysics. Heidegger felt that all of them tried to relate everything to some kind of reality or being that is assigned ultimate status. The ultimate issue, however, was more elusive.

The basic question about being itself was continually forgotten, and Heidegger tried to address it in *Being and Time*, as well as in his later works. It is what he called the ontological difference between *being* as such and *beings*. Sometimes English tries to mark this as the difference between *Being* and *beings*, by the use of a capital letter. But this is not quite enough. *Being* can be thought of as some ultimate Thing, or as something general everything has got that makes it real. Ontological difference is, rather, the difference between what makes something what it is, and what it takes for it to be there for someone to experience it for what it is. In an enigmatic phrase, Heidegger is interested in being as presencing in the presentness of beings. It is a phenomenological question rather than a metaphysical one.

Surpassing metaphysics

The question of continuity and change in Heidegger's long career as a philosopher is much discussed, in particular the extent to which, or in what way, he turned away from (to take up his own term, *die Kehre*) the earlier ontological concern with being. The continuities seem to be more in the foreground of evaluation now than perhaps in the past, while the development suggests a swing towards a greater appreciation of the openness of being.[14] Whatever the verdict, Heidegger's interest in *nothing* as a counterpoint to being gives his account of experience a depth that is particularly informative for an account of its contemplative dimension. Surpassing metaphysics is about a shift to a renewed sense of experience.

His readiness to think about the experience of being in relation to nothing rather than being as an aspect of beings is the important move. His paper 'What is metaphysics?' (1929), explicitly a complement to *Being and Time*, shifted the focus, as it were, from being to nothing.[15] He tried to consider how the thought of being arose, the questions that formed its soil. The metaphor of soil occurred again in his 'Introduction to "What is metaphysics?"', written later, in 1949.[16] By the 1950s Heidegger was concerned about technology and the way modernity had drained life of meaning by making a Nietzschean distinction between the two.[17] Here Heidegger drew a distinction between nihilism (in the Nietzschean sense) and his sense of nothing. By the end of his life, then, he came to distance himself from Nietzsche's nihilism, but there seems to be continuity in terms of his attempt to respond to it (as a problem in the human condition). A feature of his later

---

[14]Richardson, *Heidegger*, pp. 259–69, and Mark Wrathall, *Heidegger and Unconcealment*, pp. 1–34 (= Dreyfus and Wrathall (eds), *Companion*, pp. 337–57).
[15]Martin Heidegger, 'What is metaphysics?', in *Pathmarks*, edited by William McNeill (Cambridge: Cambridge University Press, 1998), pp. 82–96.
[16]Martin Heidegger, 'Introduction to "What is metaphysics?"', in *Pathmarks*, pp. 277–90.
[17]Martin Heidegger, 'On the question of being', in *Pathmarks*, pp. 291–322.

work is the variety of ways in which he tried to open up the question of being.

For Heidegger, nothing is not a denial of being; it is part of our experience of it. So, in terms of the soil in which the roots of the philosophical tree grow, it is about how (though experientially, not metaphysically) being stands out in some sense from nothing, which is perhaps conveyed in a sense of its vulnerability, its finitude. Nothing therefore plays a constructive part in what is required to live with the question of being. There is a negative aspect to it, associated with what Heidegger calls 'inauthenticity', although the 'Letter on "humanism"' shows he did not want this to be understood in the way the idea was taken by existentialists.[18] It was not about taking responsibility for giving one's life its meaning – this was the Nietzschean mistake. The challenge of authenticity was to uncover the true sense of being concealed in the negative. A constellation of terms expresses his insight, including the fragmented sense of experience in boredom (*Langeweile*) and anxiety (*Angst*, another of those words that are stronger in Heidegger's German, and which resonates with the way Kierkegaard saw the human predicament). As Heidegger puts it in 'What is metaphysics?', the question of nothing puts us in question. It represents all the difficulty in existence, its darkness, its riddling and problematic side, in contrast to which being comes to light. What feels like emptiness can be a threshold for the discovery of openness.

---

[18]Martin Heidegger, 'Letter on "humanism"', in *Pathmarks*, pp. 239–76.

Late in his work, he complements the earlier language of alienation (*Unheimlichkeit*) with the idea of finding ourselves at home (*Heim*).

In a telling phrase, Heidegger distinguishes the novelty of his approach by saying that there is 'nothing going on with being'. There is no grand narrative about reality, no implicit story about God or about human being or human reason. It just is as it is. Understanding will come by a more modest appreciation of how we are in relation to everything. The various ways Heidegger tried to express that relationship are hard to get one's head around as long as being is thought of in the way he was trying to shift.

The way this fundamental insight developed is broadly familiar. The 'turn' can be seen as an attempt to get away from the 'solid state' structure of the account he gives in *Being and Time*, to a more fluid one. In his *Contributions to Philosophy (Of the Event)*, dating from 1936–8 and first published in 1989, where he introduced the terminology of *Ereignis* that is difficult to render into English, he played with an archaic spelling of the word for being, *Seyn* instead of *Sein*.[19] He was trying to capture the historical occurrence of being, rather than a more fundamental ontology. In such an exploratory way of thinking, the term *Ereignis* (naturally translated as 'event') was more than just something that happens. In 1962 Heidegger exploited the German expression for 'there is'

---

[19]Martin Heidegger, *Contributions to Philosophy (Of the Event)*, translated by Richard Rojcewicz and Daniela Vallega-Neu (Bloomington: Indiana University Press, 2012).

(*es gibt* = 'it gives') to think in terms of what was given and what gave it.[20] The human being could be thought of in terms of receptivity; 'it' was engaged with, appropriated or, as one convention of translation puts it, 'enowned'. The human being has been displaced as the centre of the story of being. We are participants rather than protagonists. The language indicates Heidegger's increasing resistance to the Nietzschean implications of will, control and assertive power. This is most clearly captured by his use (in a conference in 1955) of the term *Gelassenheit*, which usually means 'calmness', sometimes awkwardly translated in this context as 'releasement', whose etymology speaks of 'letting be'.[21]

In the course of this developing feel for being, as opposed to beings, Heidegger gave an exegesis of various Greek words for 'being' (*einai, eon, emmenai*). Heidegger spoke in terms of 'presence'. He meant presence in a particular way, referring not to the way a thing is just solidly there, but more pregnantly, inceptively, in the way something makes its presence felt, without actually being there. It sets the conditions for everything in relation to which we have to find our way of living truthfully as human beings.

So, in a vigorous passage in *What is Called Thinking?*, from 1954, he contrasts our engagement with reality with the aggressive language of grasping (*greifen*), implicit in the

---

[20]Martin Heidegger, *On Time and Being*, translated by Joan Stambaugh (New York: Harper & Row, 1972); also in 'Letter on "humanism"', *Pathmarks*, pp. 254–5.
[21]Martin Heidegger, *Discourse on Thinking: A Translation of 'Gelassenheit'*, by John M. Anderson and E. Hans Freund (New York: Harper & Row, 1966).

usual word for 'concept' (*Begriff*), with the ideas of analysis and manipulation of data.[22] When Heidegger thinks of truth and knowledge he prefers the language of illumination. The Greek word for 'truth', *aletheia*, etymologically associated with 'unhiddenness', Heidegger glossed in terms of uncovering, and bringing to light (*Lichtung*), which has its own metaphorical associations, in German, with a clearing in a wood; the same cluster of images connect truth to terms like 'forest paths' (*Holzwege*), not properly made, but where people have worn a path in their habitual ways of getting around in the thickets.

For Heidegger, then, truth is not primarily about objective understanding of things or about dialectic articulacy, but about being able to get around and get on with life. It is a different kind of wisdom, practical not theoretic. And the point about authenticity is about truthfulness in relationships to everyone and to the world. The challenge of authenticity opens up in the recognition of finding myself in a situation where it is easy just to go along with everyone and, in an unthinking way, fall into an inattentive way of living. The notion of 'fall' is Heidegger's, without its Christian dogmatic explanation, and belongs to the metaphorical pattern surrounding 'thrown-ness'. In particular, authenticity involves a full acceptance of and integration of the truth of my being-towards-death, and the ability to see being in relation to nothing.

---

[22]Martin Heidegger, *What is Called Thinking?* (New York: Harper & Row, 1968), p. 211.

Heidegger's contribution
to a recovery

This attempt at a wide-angle view of how Heidegger envisaged moving beyond the problems he saw in metaphysics is only to consider how Heidegger's concern for being could help thinking about a contemplative dimension to experience, which in turn might contribute to a recovery of thinking about prayer. His rethinking of the issues of subjectivity and being, and especially his recognition of the place of the limits of thinking, seem to me to be aspects of thought that deserve particular attention.

Heidegger's sustained attempt to rethink the way in which human beings understand their relationship with reality is fundamental. In particular, he tries to show a way out of the Cartesian mind-set, which puts the subject in a godlike position external to the reality of the object. This permits a climb-down from the Cartesian method for sure and certain knowledge. This change in stance amounts to a fundamental resetting of experience, and allows recognition to our hesitations, our basic attitudes of trust, hope and fear, which in a context of religious faith allows a more personal and engaged relationship with God.

The key term for redefining this in *Being and Time* was called *Dasein*, where the prefix *da-* expresses the person's position in relation to things, as being-there, or being-here. It is as if knowing is about finding myself in relationship with things, which includes, then, how I am with myself. Mood is an essential part of experience; knowing is in no sense dispassionate. The word Heidegger uses is *Befindlichkeit*, which implies how I find myself (*sich befinden*). A related term he uses, *Geworfenheit*, expresses our sense of being thrown into contexts where we find ourselves. 'Thrown-ness' or 'projection' is how Heidegger preferred to expound the concept of *Ek-sistenz* (as opposed to the existentialist idea of self-created existence). By this is meant, literally, the way we 'stand out' in *Dasein* from nothing. *Dasein* is where being is disclosed – rather than something we 'see' or think about – in so far as we find ourselves standing out from, projected over, nothing. When we give up the metaphysician's cognitive distance from beings, we can get ourselves in the way of experiencing how we are in relation to the way things are presented to us.

Heidegger's different way of thinking about human being and our relationship to reality involves a different way of looking, which acknowledges a thoroughgoing participation in the world in which we find ourselves before we reflect on it as cognitive creatures. It is a way of thinking that is sensible to the way in which we find ourselves alongside other human beings. However, the language he uses for this (*Mitsein, Mitdasein* – being with; *Miteinandersein* – being in relationship with), at least in *Being and Time*, is not expounded in the terms of a proper sense of intersubjectivity. He is more concerned about the way in which conformity to a general pattern of the everyday (*das Alltägliche*) lacks authenticity.

As part of this, Heidegger understands the place of mood in human engagement. Again, he exploits the etymology to make the point: mood (*Befindlichkeit*) is about how we find ourselves (*sich befinden*). Another term associated with mood is *Stimmung*, where an English translation, 'attunement' (*stimmen* is the word for tuning, in a musical sense), suggests that more is needed than sheer passivity in order to recover from forgetfulness and to engage with the truth of being. In 'Letter on "humanism"', Heidegger speaks of being as the 'throw' that projects human beings into *Sorge*, 'care'.[23] Care is a positive way of describing the attitude needed, in Heidegger's mind, to engage with reality ('me included'). It is a way of conceiving the subjective and the objective dimensions of experience (to use the old epistemological labels) in terms of 'openness' (the metaphor suggests *Lichtung*, or 'clearing') and the ability to relate and respond while also 'letting things be' (*Gelassenheit*). The texture of this kind of thinking has a bearing on the way in which I think contemplative experience is to be understood.

The role of language and concepts comes in too, and is a second contribution. If the human being cannot stand out against reality, language cannot be an innocent medium by means of which a detached observer engages with things 'out there'. I am part of the reality I am engaged with, and the way I engage with it has a history that conditions, and also enables, my engagement. Two things follow from this. The recovery of the question of being involves a hermeneutically informed awareness of the way experience is given. Heidegger also talks

---

[23]Heidegger, 'Letter on "humanism"', in *Pathmarks*, p. 266.

of language as the way we learn to find our way around in the 'house of being', where we can learn to be (more or less) at home.

This helps justify the notorious difficulty of Heidegger's own language. Thinking has to start from the sources of our language, which means playing with compounds, etymologies, archaisms and neologisms (which can seem tendentious). It reminds us that language is not a transparent way of representing something obvious. It is a highly plastic and elastic way of finding ourselves in relation to them: how our engagement with them can change. It is similar with his interest in poetry, metaphor and the mythical categories that feature in his later writing. They are all ways of renewing a sensibility that is not conditioned by the constraints of a way of thinking that seem natural but can be part and parcel of the metaphysical forgetfulness that, for Heidegger, needs to be surpassed and overcome.

In various ways, his language is an education in understanding the limits of our thinking, its conditioning, the boundaries of our ability to make sense. It inculcates a way of pushing at those boundaries, and of trying to project a reformation of sensibility through enriching the resources of language. The power of imagination, poetic and mythic, is part of the same insight. It resonates strongly with the sense, discussed in Chapter 1, that limit experience is the place where we learn contemplative experience, the place where we experience truth not only as reality but also as a new possibility.

This is the kind of place where the later Heidegger turned to mythical and symbolic categories. They reflect his search for poetic and imaginative resources that might sustain a renewal of feeling as much as thought. They belong with his increasing interest in poets like Friedrich Hölderlin. He speaks, for instance, of the 'house of being', of our need to feel at home in a world that has been abandoned by the gods, a world that has become disenchanted. There is often a nostalgic tone in Heidegger's discussions here, of regret at the loss of a world where simple rituals have become self-conscious. Their meaning can still be appreciated, but now from the cognitive distance of people who have in one way or another moved beyond them. They have become rather quaint. Nietzsche, for his part, saw the challenge as accepting the fact and as one of learning to live bravely in the new world, taking charge of it so that it has a properly, but contemporary, human meaning. Heidegger is interesting because he can see that something vital has been lost that no amount of revaluation of values can replace. It is part of the being that is in danger of being forgotten by the wilfulness of the Nietzschean *Übermensch*.

We cannot turn the clocks back, but Heidegger is alive to the need to recover a sensibility that can appreciate meaning and value as something we inhabit, without being necessarily conscious of them as such. The dimensions of what is at stake are given in his later work by the Fourfold (*Geviert*) of sky, mortals, gods and earth. In his famous description of the way in which the temple or a bridge gather meaning around them, and constitute a world for us, he is trying to articulate the symbolic structures we need in order to live intelligently as human beings, without which our lives are incomplete.[24]

Conclusion

Nietzsche and Heidegger are two philosophers who deliberately set out to address what they saw as a fundamental and systematic error in philosophy. They saw the nihilism of the intellectual and cultural life of their respective periods as a symptom of that error, and Heidegger's work should be seen in a dialectic not just with Kant and Descartes, but also with Nietzsche. Both sought a constructive response to the problem, in markedly contrasting ways.

Similarly, I think they can help in thinking towards a new framework for contemplative prayer. This has a lot to do with the way they open up a new awareness of human subjectivity and knowledge, new approaches to the question of being and to the relation of meaning, truth and affectivity. No less important is their appreciation of human finitude, and the question of how we might retrieve an imagination of human being that is conscious of our finitude but also open to truth as a whole. The fact that they approach these questions from a position of

---

[24]The Fourfold is presented with the two examples of the temple and the bridge, respectively, in 'The origin of the work of art', in Heidegger, *Off the Beaten Track*, pp. 1–56, p. 21; 'Building, dwelling, thinking', in Heidegger, *Basic Writings*, edited by David K. Krell (London: Routledge & Kegan Paul, 1978), pp. 320–39, pp. 330–1.

disorientation, disillusionment, homelessness – with the sense of malaise that goes with this in the form of anxiety, boredom, fear – and understand the project not only as a cognitive one, but also as a challenge to a path of recovery and even of redemption, is a very significant element of the reframing that is needed.

4

Contemplative Experience

I want to follow up the approach to human experience we find in Nietzsche and Heidegger, and to bring some other sources into the story. This chapter will outline a framework for thinking about what Chapter 1 called 'contemplative experience', a term that entails no immediate theological commitments, but in relation to which I think it is easier to understand what is involved in talking specifically about contemplative prayer.

Such a framework would underlie a general account of experience; it is not about identifying certain kinds of experience that have a religious or contemplative character to them. Central to it is the way what I have called *liminality* opens up as a *threshold*. The idea of the threshold implies a 'beyond' where faith and hope (as well as love) come in and enable a movement of prayer to engage us with what is *beyond* the threshold. How this dimension opens up needs considering. The practices that support contemplative prayer can be understood as promoting the sensibility for a person to engage as much as possible with this threshold in day-to-day experience, and so to promote, in theological language, a continual awareness of the presence of God.

There are some general aspects of the human situation, touched on in the last chapter, that deserve to be mentioned. There are fundamental ethical preconditions for contemplative experience. Then something should be said about the attention that we bring to experience.

Initial ethical requirements

Contemplative experience depends on a dedication to truthfulness over fantasy and self-deception. This means being ready for work on oneself, and at least being committed to a way of life that corresponds to the search for truth implicit in contemplation. Whatever a person's interest in truth, as scientist, poet or saint, it imposes a corresponding moral and ethical demand. More is involved here than keeping rules fixed by someone else. Nietzsche's critique of conformity to an imposed moral tradition is fundamentally true. Once the moral demand loses its personal sense of being a source of transformation, and becomes a kind of respectability, or even a 'law', there is a danger that moral life becomes self-deceiving (apart from deceiving others). Truth is to be lived as a way of life, and moral virtue is the fruit of personal change and growth. That calls for an admission of our sickness and need for recovery. Contemplative life only thrives, as Nietzsche glimpsed, when a person feels to some extent on his or her own, and is prepared to take responsibility for living better. A person needs to find the value of life as a part of a commitment to truth. This is the creative Dionysian energy of life renewed by beauty and desire. It also means being able to go against the grain of what is usually encouraged and applauded by a society in the name of integrity or truthfulness.

But to think of truthfulness even in these terms is to turn Nietzsche on his head! Contemplative experience recognizes that truthfulness is a matter of obedience, not of self-assertion. To that extent Nietzsche got it exactly wrong! The obedience needed is not to the interests of another but to the truth, to the way my life is or needs to be in order to flourish. Heidegger's work of reversal is fundamental here, from his earliest analysis of human being as *Dasein* to his later sense of the need for *Gelassenheit*. But there are two other elements about contemplative experience that Nietzsche helps to articulate. One is the need, not only to recover from the malaise of any bad thinking, but also to recognize that this requires radical change and transformation. For him, contemplative living belongs to a transformative vision of the world. The 'overman', or *Übermensch*, belongs to a new world beyond the present, but this is probably best thought of in eschatological rather than in historical terms. In this ultimate world, truth is to be realized as a fullness of life, in its Dionysiac, ecstatic-creative-redemptive vitality. If Nietzsche underestimated the horror of the human condition and the nature of the redemption needed, his perspective is a reminder of the importance of the eschatological dimension of Christian soteriology. Contemplation needs to be engaged in the costly work of redemption and commitment to some kind of eschatological vision in terms of which we can re-envision the fullness of life. Nietzsche objected to the other-worldliness of the Christianity he knew. This world is not good enough, but escape is not the answer. Nietzsche was calling for change.

Second, Nietzsche challenges our fantasies about power and our need for God. He criticized the Christianity he knew for its addiction to a false god and to a false understanding of the human condition. His critique is a continual call to attention when we are confronted with what Jesus represents. If *he* is what divine power means, then we habitually miss the point. The way we understand power, the way we try to control things and justify the use of violence, the way we set about rationalizing our environment and commodifying it for our own use and enjoyment, the way we ignore things (and people) . . . they are all symptoms of a religious perspective based on God as creator and ruler, to be sure, but not of an appreciation of how Jesus changed that perspective on God. It is a perspective where it is dangerously easy to see ourselves as entitled to appropriate quasi-divine authority to our own projects and aspirations. When Heidegger saw the links between Descartes and modern technology, he was not just making a philosophical point. The mistake of onto-theology is not an argument for atheism – we just replace one god with another, unless there is a change of heart, unless we learn to live honestly and without fantasies.

Heidegger also reminds us of the danger of fantasizing about being. Nothing is really going on with being; there is no big story about *being*.[1] What is needed is more modesty and less over-inflated ambition.[2] A corollary, then, to accepting the 'death of god', is to accept our finitude and befriend it. This is harder than we like. Heidegger states clearly that being is essentially finite. Rather than with the Absolute, it rubs shoulders with nothing.[3] The insight is a consequence of Kant's critique of pure reason, where the field of reason is limited to the *phenomenon*. A significant corollary of this was Kant's recognition that faith has a proper place in our understanding, and that its function is distinct from the ordinary operation of reason.[4]

Christian ideas about contemplation can turn into fantasies about tops of grandiose mountains. We do not bear in mind the actual conditions in which, in the biblical sources of this image, God actually revealed himself to people like Moses, Elijah or Jesus. We look for the high ground rather than the little way, of a Thérèse of Lisieux. We forget about our hardness of heart, our idolatry and our need for repentance. We think, with suitable equipment and technology, that we can tough out the fierceness of the mountains and deserts of the spiritual journey. We forget the dispossession and dereliction of the journey to Calvary.

---

[1]Martin Heidegger, 'Nietzsche's word: "God is dead"', in *Off the Beaten Track*, p. 197.
[2]Heidegger, 'Letter on "humanism"', in *Pathmarks*, pp. 255–6, and esp. p. 268.
[3]Heidegger, 'What is metaphysics?', in *Pathmarks*, p. 94.
[4]Fergus Kerr makes the connections with Kant, in relation to Stanley Cavell, in his discussion of Wittgenstein as a 'friend of finitude', in *Work on Oneself: Wittgenstein's Philosophical Psychology* (Washington, DC: Catholic University of America Press, 2008), pp. 99–100.

The intriguing fact is that the greatest literature in the genre of desert spirituality works under no illusions about the kind of truthfulness that prayer and a life of faith require.[5] The fantasy is challenged as soon as a person seriously undertakes the journey that it involves.

This is one way of saying that the 'nothing' in nihilism has to be taken seriously. In *Being and Time* Heidegger thinks of being as being-towards-death. I am not sure this is as prominent in all his discussion of nothing. He associates the haunting sense of our orientation to death with anxiety and boredom, and so with the experiential field of liminality; it also plays into our tendency to inauthentic against authentic being. But there is a deeper problem than the emptiness in our experience of the world. Nothing is more than a background for the possibilities of being. Death and the fear of it warp our perception of things and interfere with our engagement with life more profoundly than that. Nietzsche at least does not shy away from our need for salvation and transformation. He understands that our moral life has to be reconstituted, eschatologically, from beyond.

Attention and contemplative experience

These ethical considerations form, as it were, the base of the framework, what enables it to stand firm on the ground of

---

[5]Belden C. Lane, *The Solace of Fierce Landscapes: Exploring Desert and Mountain Spirituality* (Oxford: Oxford University Press, 2007), is a fine contribution to the literature of 'desert spirituality'.

human life. The requirement for truthfulness goes further. It also means laying aside personal interests. The engagement with the truth that is beyond me must be disinterested. Heidegger's notion of truth as openness to being is instructive here. In particular, his discussion of truth in terms of light and of woodland clearings shows how it can be understood in relation to finitude. We are never in a position to know completely; we have to follow a path, which becomes clear (more or less) only as we proceed. And things become progressively clear as we move along, even though we only ever see them from a point of view, and never as a whole. What is important is the attention we give.

An example is when we look at a picture. Initially we just see it and recognize it, as if that was that. What strikes us initially may well be something that says more about us than about the picture, something in the way it reflects our experience or aspirations. Our attention has to move beyond our personal preoccupations; it needs to engage with the picture itself. We might ask ourselves what strikes us and how, and let the work itself teach us how to look at it. That may mean a change of attitude, a conversion of mind and heart. We have to let the picture be. What matters is how the picture 'works'; we need to enter the world the picture creates and try to see it as a whole. It is a gradual process, and it is a process more like a conversation than a speech, but that is how a picture 'speaks to us'. In the process we have learned to pay attention.

This is a hermeneutic process. Once we have begun to pay attention, dispassionate looking does not leave us untouched. It lets the object of our experience take the initiative, as it were, in disclosing itself. It works in the way in which we are able to let ourselves be surprised and challenged by what we see. We find ourselves invited to new ways of looking, and to new ways of learning to look at everything in the light of that experience. In this context, it is also uncontroversial, however strange it is to reflect on, that what works for one person will not for another; a painting can have different 'conversations' with each, which can enable a worthwhile conversation between the two people as well.

Simone Weil talks about attention with an eye not only to its academic but also to its spiritual value in *Waiting on God*, in a discussion about school studies dating to 1942, where she speaks of disinterestedness.[6] She notes that it is not will but desire that directs our intelligence. For her, desire is what gives the natural orientation of a person's mind towards God. It is an effort because of our resistance to that true desire. For all her talk of desire and love, she distinguishes, surprisingly, between attention and the 'heart's warmth'.[7] The important point is her observation that, however it is a matter of the intelligence, attention means suspending thought, not to be unthinking, but to let it be free of our agendas and concerns. There needs to be a shift in the centre of gravity of our attention, away from

---

[6]Simone Weil, 'Reflections on the right use of school studies with a view to the love of God', in *Waiting on God*, translated by Emma Crauford (Glasgow: Collins, 1983), pp. 66–76.

[7]For a note of criticism of her approach to disinterestedness, see Rowan Williams, 'Simone Weil and the necessary non-existence of God', in his *Wrestling with Angels*, edited by Mike Higton (London: SCM Press, 2007), pp. 203–27.

us to the object of our attention, so that it can disclose itself. The most precious things must be waited for; they cannot be found, and were we to try to look for them we would only find false goods whose falsehood, ironically, we would not be able to discern.

The point that emerges is the need to cultivate a kind of interest in something that lets it be, not one that is shaped by our ego. An essential part of achieving this is a kind of suspension of thought, a kind of blankness in what we bring to experience or rather openness to it, disinterested but not dispassionate. Passion, as well as desire, plays a part.

Another metaphor is listening. To listen well we need to be aware of the voices in our own heads, our own interests, all that we bring to the conversation that is irrelevant to what the other person has to say. Obviously, complete detachment makes conversation impossible. Personal contact entails the presence of people who have a lot else going on in their heads. But acknowledgement of what is not relevant, and acceptance of it for what it is, helps us to set it aside for the sake of the other person. And, more than that, a properly active listening on our part can help another person articulate better what needs to be said as well as understood.[8]

---

[8] A useful collection of papers is in A. Liégeois *et al.*, *'After You!' Dialogical Ethics and the Pastoral Counselling Process*, Bibliotheca Ephemeridum Theologicarum Lovaniensium 258 (Leuven: Peeters, 2013), especially those by L. Lipari, 'The vocation of listening: the other side of dialogue', pp. 15–36, and M. Riemslagh, 'Asymmetric reciprocity in pastoral dialogue: reflections on effective pastoral counselling inspired by the thought of Lévinas and Buber', pp. 139–58.

Liminality

On the basis of these initial considerations we can turn to the central structure in the framework. This is the relationship between liminality and threshold: what opens up a limit experience to something that invites us beyond?

Liminality relates to a particular person's engagement in experience. It is a situation where the usual structure of beliefs, desires and intentions with which I make practical sense of the world, and make it my life, are compromised or break down. It is as if I wake up to find myself in a place where everyone is speaking a foreign language. I recognize everything going on, at least in a general kind of way. But, out of the blue, I do not know what they are saying, or how to respond. There is an immediate content to what I experience, but I cannot engage with any meaning; the points of reference I expect to have available are not there. That is to say, there is some kind of dissonance between it and the way in which I am trying to engage with it.

In normal cases of doubt and uncertainty, I know how to ask questions, and keep myself open for more experience. I have learned appropriate ways of changing my beliefs to adjust to the unknown or the surprising; that is how my understanding develops. But in liminality something deeper is going on; some fundamental structure in the way I find meaning is being challenged; and, most profoundly, I am myself put in question. For, in relation to this, I do not know where I am or how to find myself. It is what Michael Sells calls an anarchic moment and there is no saying what will come out of it, how it will affect me in the longer term.

The anarchic moment lies in the way subjectivity in what Sells calls the meaning event is shaken, and the equilibrium, as it were, in the relationship between subject and object shifts, so that 'I' am no longer 'in charge'. This is the reason for Sells' preferring to talk of experience as a meaning event, except that in this case the meaning is not there in the usual way. An obvious analogy for the shift in equilibrium is the experience of falling in love. The verb bears the point out. I am no longer standing on my own ground. In the development of a proper relationship of love between two people, each has to give the other ground, and find an intersubjectivity that sustains their own personal autonomy as well. The point I want to note is that this involves some fundamental shifts to the centre of gravity of a person's subjectivity.

Religious conversion is another example. There can be a long process of slippage and loosening of convictions before a resolution is found. Anarchy can be a long time in the making; but we are often scarcely aware of what is going on until it all gives way. After the event, perhaps we can put the pieces more or less intelligibly together. However, we learn to tell the story later on so that the pieces fit reasonably together; we do not have that perspective or intelligibility at the time.

Even in liminal experience, reading our experience is a hermeneutic affair. We bring to it a set of beliefs and values to interpret it, which are the fruit of our previous understanding and concerns. It is never just up to us, and this is made forcibly clear in an anarchic moment; but there is a dialogue between what we bring and what we find. The subjective and the objective go hand in hand. There is a relationship, and Nietzsche was right to see that values are not simply inherent in the objectivity of things. But Heidegger was right to criticize his conclusion that we can and must impose our values on them. Liminal experience disrupts the usual dynamic in this process of understanding, and we have to let things unfold and teach us how to make sense of them. But it is a meaning event. Sheer passivity or pure consciousness is not enough for us to make sense of it; we need a more attentive, active listening and looking, a greater readiness to set aside what we bring to it; it calls for a real openness and receptivity to things, a letting them be, that can be called contemplative.

Various elements of our subjectivity, such as intentions and interests, moods and passions, all things that hold sway over the attention we bring to experience, become sources of interference in a liminal situation. Sometimes, but not always, the circumstances are enough to shake us out of them. What Simone Weil teaches is that the kind of disinterestedness that promotes the necessary contemplative openness is born of a desire to understand, which we are able to hold onto in spite of all that seems to undermine it. That fundamental desire expresses our trust in even the unknown and incomprehensible to be a source of truth and of life. The place of faith in being able to address this kind of experience is crucial – a fundamental trust that the truth is *there* in a reality that eludes me. To acknowledge the place of faith is also to acknowledge a place for hope, the hope that understanding can be reached, and that there is a way of living more fully by learning from the elusiveness of the experience. Weil speaks of desire that is a core part of the human dynamic; desire carries a person beyond the present. She readily understood the movement of desire to be intrinsically orientated towards God, and perhaps the most important element in liminal experience is how a person understands desire as having a direction. Does core human desiring reach out for fulfilment in something 'beyond' – and how is that 'beyond' experienced – or is desire necessarily confined to finitude and frustrated by it? This is the crux in our experience of liminality; it is what turns it into experience of a threshold.

Intentionality of awareness

Liminal experience, and especially in contemplative prayer, raises important issues about intentionality. Some of them have already been indicated in what has been said about pure consciousness; and Sells' preference for meaning events is prompted by a desire to avoid the problem. Within the limits of the present discussion, only some rather tentative thoughts can be developed.

Looking at a view, remembering my trip to Venice, looking forwards to going home all include similarly comprehensive intentional objects. Under the heading 'trip to Venice' I will call a series of things to mind, in no particular order, and in different ways on different occasions. Indeed, I can bring to mind something I had forgotten, or never paid attention to before. The general point is that, even if there is a specific content to the mental object 'trip to Venice' at any time, it is not any specific content that determines what it is for me to remember the visit. The mental object does not have a decisive form.

Looking at nothing in particular is a more interesting case. My attention plays over a scene, inadvertently (a significant modifier) noticing this or that, but without any intention (in the other sense of the word) of thinking about anything. It ranges free. In some way I am glad to 'take it all in', or there may be too much to take in all at once. But it is not possible for 'all of it' to be a mental object, in the sense that it is all the object of my attention. However I specify the mental act, the 'all' has to be put under some kind of limiting description. I gaze at the landscape; I listen to the cry of birds over the distant sound of traffic in the background. And there is a real sense in which I would say I am not thinking of anything. There is an openness in my attention that cannot be given a propositional form in terms of mental objects. What I am doing goes beyond the logic of how it gets put into words. Furthermore, my engagement with a situation is more complex than simply the work of five discrete senses; it can be a deeply emotional experience that engages my whole person, and affects my way of seeing myself, including my hopes, desires and intentions. 'Musing' is a good word for this. The muses are the channels of inspiration. This can be a creative process in the course of which I find an insight, a way of putting things, a way of seeing and understanding.

Contemplative awareness seems to be where the intentionality of the activity is indeterminate. It can be a state of heightened attentiveness, but attention cannot be indeterminate; there must be an object. There is a logical tension here, which eases as we see how unimportant the objects of attention can be, as the attentiveness of the contemplative state of mind ranges freely. Attention is, as it were, taken over by the sense of a bigger perspective; its more particular cognitive activity becomes largely incidental to a different kind of intentionality. For example, I do hear the birds and the traffic, but my engagement in the scene is not at that level; a different kind of mindfulness is involved – less about trying to take charge of the situation cognitively, more about trying to let a different kind of experience open up. It may not even be about trying to understand anything; it would be enough just to enjoy it, to 'drink it in'. The 'it' is purely grammatical, to help the verb function. It might be about acknowledging a deeper sense of relationship to it, where I can find myself. 'Its' *thereness* discloses my *hereness*. In other words, it is not really about an object at all. Heidegger's conception of *Ereignis* has a good resonance with this kind of thing.

What happens in liminal experience? Heidegger's interest in the limits of experience, and the way language and symbol play a particular role there, is particularly significant. In 'What is metaphysics?', Heidegger observes that it is the strangeness of beings that forces nothingness on us, where we have a sense of

being left hanging, or held out into nothing. It is in this experience, or 'manifestness', of nothing that we approach beings; it is in
relation to the sense of nothing (boredom or anxiety, our mood)
that we find ourselves, or attune ourselves (*Stimmung*).[9]
Liminality, then, is the experience of the strangeness of beings.
Where Heidegger speaks of finding ourselves in relation to
nothingness, there is a limit of thinking where the intentionality
of experience implodes. This is an anarchic moment, in Sells'
terminology. It is not so unusual that we cannot understand a
situation, but here we do not even know how to respond to our
experience or to relate to what is going on. Intentionality breaks
down because of the unknown. We have reached a limit, an edge
in experience – which is the shape its intentionality takes.

As an intentional object, an edge is not only a boundary; it
marks a disruption. You can go over the edge, as it were, but
it will be different, and ignorance of the possibilities of being
able to negotiate the change is a restraint. What defines an edge
is that of which it is an edge; it has no relationship to what is
beyond. As far as there is an edge, what is beyond it has to be
left open. And yet the edge presupposes that beyond to which
it gives no clue. It is an unknown implicit in the intentionality
of my awareness of the edge, and in liminal experience it is the
implicitly unknown, that to which I cannot relate, that captures
my attention and makes demands on me.

But the edge often turns up as a blank, a blank wall or a
dead end. The frustration in this is not only that I do not know

---

[9]Heidegger, 'What is metaphysics?', in *Pathmarks*, pp. 88, 91, 94.

what is beyond it, but that I cannot get round it or find my way through. In this situation, desire is pulling me beyond the limits of my intentionality towards an openness of which I have, in fact, no idea. That is what makes it a blank wall. I think that the apophatic tradition helps indicate that it is not so much a case of non-intentional awareness, but a situation where the intentionality does not really specify what is going on. For practical purposes it becomes irrelevant, and what is really going on needs to be approached from a different perspective.

Central to what liminal experience calls into question is the way I find myself. The *Befindlichkeit* and affectivity, which Heidegger saw was fundamental to experience, becomes prominent in liminal experience, where the sense of my being is more than ever conscious of its relationship to nothing. So, in contemplative prayer, the practices of silence and stillness expose the tangle of thoughts and desires in my *Befindlichkeit*, and the experience of those who pray contemplatively over a long time is of a growth in wisdom and discernment, not only in relation to themselves, but in relation to their relationships to others and in their sensitivity to the whole of life.[10] This

[10]Sarah Coakley, in 'Prayer as divine propulsion: an interview with Sarah Coakley', *The Other Journal: An Intersection of Theology and Culture*, part 1 (20 December 2012), http://theotherjournal.com/2012/12/20/prayer-as-divine-propulsion-an-interview-with-sarah-coakley/; Part 2 (27 December 2012), http://theotherjournal.com/2012/12/27/prayer-as-divine-propulsion-an-interview-with-sarah-coakley-part-ii (accessed on 6 October 2014); compare also Sarah Coakley, *Powers and Submissions: Spirituality, Philosophy and Gender* (Oxford: Blackwell, 2002), especially chs 1 and 2, pp. 3–54, which discuss the 'contemplative matrix' in terms of vulnerability.

does not explain how God comes into the account. But at least the first step could be thought of in these terms, that liminal experience forces me to see myself from a different point of view. A situation where I am wondering how I find myself opens up the question of where I am, and my relationship to everything else. From this point of view, aspects of life that I perhaps even avoid thinking about can become more significant. Liminal experience not only forces a change in the structure of beliefs with which I meet the world, but also in my understanding of my desiring and what might satisfy it. I do not know what its satisfaction is, but I will be better able to know it when I find it. This is a critical step.

Intentionality in contemplative prayer

The key difficulty is how to understand the idea of contact with God in prayer. God can be a mental object under some description or name. I can think of him in this kind of way, and formal prayers usually even offer the description; but contemplative prayer traditionally envisages some more direct form of contact, analogous to perception. And here experience is generally quite the opposite, a blank. It is like falling in love with what Dom John Chapman called a blank.[11] This catches the emotional paradox, but I think it needs a little unpacking. I do not love the blank wall, of course. But I am aware that what

---

[11]See Chapter 1, n. 2. It is telling that Chapman talks about will and not love.

has brought me there is love and the search for my heart's desire. And the blank is all there is. The intentionality is frustrated: what is my heart's desire? I do not know it until I find it, but how do I carry on looking? I can go no further, at least until something fundamental shifts, usually *in me*, and I find myself trying to move forwards but in profoundly unfamiliar territory, as far as the next blank!

The dynamic of ignorance and personal change is central to contemplative prayer. Chapman used the idea of 'thinking about nothing in particular' as a way of talking about how God is the intentional object ('which is God, of course'.) The consideration of this in the last section again suggests that this is too quick an answer to the problem. Apart from the fact that (as a description of how to set about praying) it obscures the distinction between wanting God and daydreaming, it simply avoids facing the question of how God enters into the intentionality of what I am doing. As the previous comments suggested, thinking about nothing in particular is a way of describing a kind of openness of attention in which my intentions and desires come to the surface, but it remains to say something about how what is beyond the limit of my thinking can make his presence felt – that is to say, how liminal experience can become a threshold for the discovery of God.

To talk of a blank is paradoxical; there is too much going on in my mind most of the time, which has nothing to do with my attempt to pray. That is no different from when I am thinking about something but have a lot else on my mind. So it is necessary to focus my attention, and this is an important part of contemplative practice. But on what? There is a paradox here. I may use words, images, devotions. The means are not the intentional object in the ulterior sense, as it were; they are stepping stones, transitional objects, in some way to be left behind at an intentional level, even though the action or the words carry on in the background. As such, they help to disengage the mind from specific intentionality to allow it to be open to an intentionality where we have very little to focus on, or to hold it. The meditative practices that help to cultivate silence and mindfulness educate our sensibility for the attention that is needed.

Liminal experience as a threshold of prayer

Liminality presents us with the unknown; however familiar we supposed the situation to be, what hits us is the strangeness of what confronts us. The challenge is how open we can be in response to otherness. The way we respond to it has a lot to do with the way in which the limit can become a threshold experience. In this case, we can cross the threshold into a new way of seeing things, a way of living that can be enriched by the experience. There is a shift about which some more needs to be said.

In so far as liminality presents us with a religious dimension, the threshold is different, because there is no way across. The ontological difference between creature and creator does not allow it. The metaphor is hard to ground. However, the experience of prayer suggests that the blank wall is not the end of the story. It becomes a threshold and not a blank wall. On the one hand, when we pray, we are aware of how our capacity to understand runs out, in spite of the desire that draws our attention. At the same time our desire, supported by faith and hope, looks towards the unknowable for fulfilment. In Heidegger's terminology, it is how we feel left hanging over nothing, where the ground of being and understanding comes to an edge or abyss. And yet the dynamic of desire in faith and hope is what makes us pay attention to even what eludes being a mental object in more than a formal sense. It draws our attention across a threshold, even though as a threshold it marks a limit to our understanding we cannot cross.

At this point a philosophical account of contemplative prayer has to mark time. But it should not be surprising because this is where we have to observe the threshold between philosophy and theology. But we can say that the limit in experience is one where we find the ontological difference between creator and creature, and where it would be impossible to import the idea of God as some kind of foundation of reality that would allow us to cross. It does not follow that God is unreal; it means that without faith we have no means of engaging cognitively with him, or of thinking out how prayer is in any sense a union of love and knowledge. This is where we need theology to teach us. It is also where further philosophical questions arise.

Threshold and otherness

With that caveat, there is another line of thought to be considered which connects with the observations about attention and desire. It is about the 'other'. I have suggested that the strangeness of the experience of liminality is felt as alienation. The strangeness of the experience arises from a sense of otherness, and the alienation arises from the sense of how that otherness puts me in question. My sense of this experience is that I am forced back on my own sense of subjectivity, and how the questions of who I am, and what makes me who I am, become live questions – about the *who*, not the *what* – in my sense of identity. And yet, the obvious sense of personal identity, of being the subject that asks the question, is not a satisfactory answer. It leaves me acutely aware of a sense of exposure, of there not being what I need to give a secure response, or even, securely, to be the response to my own question. At the heart of this sense of alienation my experience is one where I recognize my sense of subjectivity as one I am given from the other, and in this sense of subjectivity I become aware of the personal character of the other as the source of my own being, in a relationship of mutual presence. This is what I understand to be how the shift takes place in liminality to a sense of the limit now as a threshold.

This experience of otherness is distinct from what I understand Hegel or Lévinas to have meant by the term. In Hegel, it seems to me that the other is approached from the subject's point of view and engaged with on the subject's terms, whatever exchange then takes place, only the person's own appropriation of the experience promotes growth and change. It all depends on the subject. However, in my understanding of liminal experience, the subject's point of view is compromised. The situation is therefore more like what Emmanuel Lévinas is trying to describe, where the other is an absolute who confronts me in such a way as to rupture my sense, as a subject, of being able (ultimately) to take command of reality from *my point of view*. In engaging with another and recognizing him or her as another *person*, my own point of view has no bearing on the other's being another subject, the person I need to engage with as another subject.

Lévinas catches the absoluteness in this sense of the threshold, but pays little attention to the equilibriums that are involved in intersubjectivity. Any personal encounter has to do with what is alien to me; it is not a relationship between subject and object where I can presume some cognitive authority as an observer; it is a relationship between subject and subject. I have to wait on the word of the other; I have to be open to the other for any mutual basis for a relationship. In so far as there is a basis for this relationship, the limit becomes a threshold over which I can pass. However, I do not pass over into the other's subjectivity; while the other remains 'other' ontologically, the relationship is one where one is open to the other and this invites a response of mutuality. If this is accepted, the engagement makes mutual knowledge possible (in love) while respecting the ontological limits.

In the liminal experience of prayer, I suggest that there is a limit I cannot cross which is more fundamental than the threshold that separates me from another human subject. This threshold puts me in question more fundamentally than any human relationship. But even here there is a relationship, and the possibility of an exchange. This is fundamentally what I think happens in prayer, where we can and cannot cross the ontological limit between creature and creator, but where my recognition of God's otherness as an openness and invitation to love constitutes a threshold I negotiate in prayer. In the framework I am exploring, prayer would be a particular way of negotiating liminality in experience, where the openness to the other is in fact discovered as openness to God.

More is involved than the *otherness* of the other, even though that categorical difference is fundamental. The other does not displace me entirely, however much his otherness forces me to recognize my finitude. The threshold is a place of *relationship*. Not only is the confrontation of my subjectivity by the other important, and marks a limit to my experience, but our mutual relationship is just as important, which is mediated by our intersubjectivity. The balance between the two depends on the relationship, and some relationships are more intersubjective than others! What they all show is how I discover myself in relation to the other; and it is the otherness, not the likeness, of the other that enables this. Indeed I discover myself in relation to another as being given back to myself (thanks to the relationship) by the other as I could not otherwise be.

The way liminal experience can open up a threshold is, in some way, similar to this. That is to say, the experience of liminality, which affords me a heightened, deepened, enriched sense of the truth of my own being (however mysterious and even challenging that is) is an experience of a relationship to an otherness that enables my personal being, my personhood as such. This cannot be an *argument* for God's existence. But it is a structure in experience that is a help to understanding how it is possible to cross a threshold of liminality between the finite and the infinite. Personal reality opens up personhood; it sets up the right kind of existential space.

It is a way of understanding a person's experience in prayer, of understanding the experience as prayer. The suggestion is basically that in prayer I find myself engaging with an other in relation to whom I find myself being given back to myself as I could not otherwise know myself to be. The abiding mystery in prayer seems to me to be the centrality of this kind of personal dimension or relationship, even though I have no other way of seeing myself in relation to this person; the unknowability, the sheer elusiveness is about all I can point to in order to name the person 'behind' it as God. Obviously, much more needs to be said, and more than I think can ever be said. But, for the moment, I think this is a basic experience of prayer, and implicit in it is the sense of there being a limit to my experience that can open up as a threshold.

5

Knowing and Unknowing

Discussions of contemplative prayer have generally affirmed that contemplation is, however mysteriously, a way of growing in the knowledge and love of God. As a personal relationship between the human being and God, this relationship involves more than our minds; it is a thing that engages us, heart and soul – body and spirit too. This is all a way of saying that faith is more than just a rational act, in the sense of being only a matter of logic and propositions. One of the strengths of the so-called traditional framework was the place given to the intellect as an intuitive and non-discursive power, and even, influenced by Plato, of erotic love.

This understanding of the mind was lost in the story I have outlined, and the possibility of knowing God, and of faith, as an *intelligent* response of love to love, needs to be retrieved in a very different intellectual environment. The path I have been trying to pick out is, paradoxically, one that starts from the disorientating experience of loss of meaning, a blank, where thinking comes to a stop.[1] But in thinking out what might be going on there, I find that the knowing, in some way, still carries on. A different approach to rationality is called for, that is, addressing a new starting point for knowing. Obviously, what distinguishes religious faith at this point is the particular way in which a person finds that understanding has dawned.

The approach I have taken owes much to people who have been critical of the presiding rationalism of Descartes or the Enlightenment. Pascal, Kierkegaard and Dostoevsky, on the other hand, put the emphasis on faith, and emphasize the paradox in faith, the place of commitment and trust, the sheer freedom of the will rather than reason. They have often been seen as irrationalist. Nietzsche, obviously, as an atheist, thought faith was irrational but, more than that, argued that the will (to power) was the foundation for a necessary revaluation of values in order to exorcize God from his position in thought. Heidegger is interesting because he connects a critique of rationalism with the search for a new way of thinking about being, a new starting point for awareness.

The implication of the path taken so far is that contemplation now has to be approached in terms of human finitude. It cannot, as simply as in the past, be assumed to be the basis for a transcendence of the material and human to the spiritual and divine. Absolute reality is no longer so readily accessible an idea.

---

[1] The phrase is from Ludwig Wittgenstein, *Zettel*, 2nd edn (Oxford: Blackwell, 1991), §314.

A term that serves the purpose well here is that of 'unknowing'. It comes from the English text *The Cloud of Unknowing*, and its anonymous author finds it in the apophatic tradition of Pseudo-Dionysius the Areopagite. It is a cognitive relation, but in a unique way, which this chapter attempts to explore. It is to be contrasted to other positions that assert, for instance, that all language about God is necessarily a human construction and is ultimately about ourselves. Both are unsatisfactory. Our engagement with reality goes deeper than knowledge and words, and it has to be cognitive for it to be love.

Postmodern scepticism

Unknowing is not scepticism about knowledge. I do not believe a methodical scepticism about knowledge or truth is justified by the challenges postmodernism fairly raises against the grand narratives of Enlightenment and modern philosophy. It is possible to reject the Cartesian separation of subject and object without being obliged to the view that objective knowledge entails stepping outside the linguistic environment in which alone we can think and speak. Scientific rationality can go too far, but it can still have a valid rationale. The human subject is fallible and our efforts to tell the truth are provisional, but it does not follow that there is no truth to be sought or known. These are the parameters for a middle way.

Similarly, we need to be hermeneutically self-aware, and recognize how language and concepts are themselves the fruit of traditions and a particular cultural formation before they are ever used to speak about the way we see things. But the crucial issue is to recognize that there is an external constraint on my ability to speak the truth, and that the concept of truth still functions as an authority over my use of language. The form of metaphysical account of reality that goes with this idea of truth is controversial; but it can be accepted that making a statement is a more complex activity than simply pointing to something 'out there' and saying something about it. Language is not always completely transparent to the world out there, but a cautious realism can be based on the belief that language offers access to something other than itself.[2]

Underlying this is a question about trust, whether we can trust experience, and accept that experience can be understood without being conditioned and compromised by the position and the means we have at our disposal to put it into words. The question is whether language articulates truth about the world, or whether it can only distort what is said so as to make it no more than a statement about the speaker. We appreciate how often assertions of interest are disguised in factual discourse, and how reasoning can be a manipulative rhetoric of power, but it does not follow that what we say can only be an expression of our culture and prejudices. To be sure, people distort things; but the logic of language makes a useful distinction between the way it allows people to express

---

[2]See Rowan Williams, "'Religious realism": on not quite agreeing with Don Cupitt', in *Wrestling with Angels*, pp. 228–54.

themselves and the possibility of saying something that can claim to be true for everyone.

An epistemological fallacy

The scepticism that is involved here seems to me to depend on accepting the distinction between subject (knower) and object (known) on Descartes' terms – not as a logical distinction, but as a metaphysical one between two distinct substances, mind and body. This sets the knower outside and apart from the material reality that is the object of knowledge. It served for Descartes' answer to the sceptical problem. But it is not the only way to ground epistemology. For the purposes of what I am calling 'contemplative experience', it is possible to lower the metaphysical stakes.

A logical distinction between subject and object only states what is implicit in the grammar, say, in 'I recognize the situation'. Verifying what I see as what I think it to be is another matter. But there are various procedures for doing this. I can be systematically deluded; my perception and cognitive ability may be impaired. There are ways of establishing either. But the basic underlying principle seems sensible, that the way we engage with the world around us enables us to know it in the only sense of 'know' that matters. The corollary, *pace* Descartes, is the importance of our being part of the reality we know and not external to it. This means that the relationship between subject and object, not the distinction, is what warrants the logic of subject and object. This relationship is what constitutes the whole notion of consciousness.

It means that this relationship is prior to knowledge and that knowledge is not the basic way in which we are related to everything else. What might be called an 'epistemological fallacy', that our relationship to, or participation in reality is fundamentally about knowledge, is a direct consequence of the Cartesian way of conceiving our situation, and in principle it sets subject and object apart. Once that distinction has been given up, it is easier to see how knowledge, or trying to know, depends on innumerable patterns of behaviour and 'forms of life' – Wittgenstein must surely be right here – that most elementally express the way we are the beings we are, and which are more or less communicative in character, a matter of language.

Heidegger says something similar when he speaks of *Dasein*. In fact, it is central to a phenomenological approach to experience. He unpacks his ontological concern in terms of our practical engagement in the world (*Besorgen*) in which 'concern' (*Sorge*) is given a high profile. It reflects his sense of the question of being as one that opens up in relation to nothing. This is scarcely the whole story of our engagement in things and with people; the full range of our affectivity, with our moods, emotions and desires, plays a crucial part in the way we find ourselves in the midst of things and in relation to others, and recognition of this has a particular bearing on the role of our affectivity in contemplative prayer. They are primary ways in which we find ourselves part of all that there is. They express our underlying attitudes and capacity for faith and doubt, for truthfulness and for deception and error as well as vanity and wishful thinking (which is not thinking at all). Aristotle appreciated the fact when he showed how human virtue, both moral and intellectual, rested on settled dispositions of character and on our way of coming to grips with the world (what he called *orexis*).

Acknowledgement and trust

Philosophers like Stanley Cavell and Hilary Putnam have developed some salient ideas of Wittgenstein's *On Certainty* in the same direction. Wittgenstein is clear that a language game is only possible on the basis of trust. He talks about a grasp (*Zugreifen*) that is not a knowing (*Wissen*) but gives sureness (*Sicherheit*).[3] By knowing, Wittgenstein has in mind something that can be rationally grounded (*Grund*) even as a language game;[4] it presumes on more than a subjective certainty, and is based on an understanding, a proof. But language is not grounded on ratiocination; it arises from our animal condition as human beings, even as it distinguishes us from animals.[5] So he speaks of the 'thereness' of a life, and of the way language just is part of that, without being a matter of reasoning

---

[3]Ludwig Wittgenstein, *On Certainty*, edited by G. E. M. Anscombe and George Henrik von Wright (Oxford: Blackwell, 1975), §§509, 511.
[4]Wittgenstein, *On Certainty*, §560.
[5]Wittgenstein, *On Certainty*, §475.

(*vernünftig*).[6] Earlier he had reflected how difficult it is to get an insight into the groundlessness of our believing (as a matter of rationality); he glosses this in terms of the propositional form that experience takes (*Erfahrungsaussagen*).[7] This structure of belief rests not on seeing the truth of a proposition but on our engagement in life, our acting (*Handeln*). If truth rests on grounds, the ground is neither true nor false; it is just there.[8] But it is not just a matter of action; there is a perspective, an outlook. In a later paragraph, he uses the word *Betrachtung*, translated as 'way of looking at things'. It is a way of seeing things as a whole, a scaffolding (supporting what?), which we learn, and which can change.[9] It seems that Wittgenstein is reluctant to use a more direct verb for vision because of the propositional burden it carries, but nonetheless envisages our engagement as intelligent, mindful, acknowledging. This is where the notion of contemplative experience comes in.

In developing Wittgenstein's ideas, Putnam and Cavell are both resisting a sceptical challenge from people like Richard Rorty to a certain kind of realist, that language 'goes all the way down'.[10] The varieties of realism do not need analysis here.[11]

---

[6]Wittgenstein, *On Certainty*, §559: 'It is there, like our life.'

[7]Wittgenstein, *On Certainty*, §166.

[8]Wittgenstein, *On Certainty*, §§204–5; see also *Culture and Value*, edited by G. H. von Wright (Oxford: Blackwell, 1980), p. 31 (a comment from 1937): 'In the beginning was the deed'; language is a 'refinement'.

[9]Wittgenstein, *On Certainty*, §211.

[10]Richard Rorty, *Consequences of Pragmatism*, pp. xxx, xxxv.

[11]Hilary Putnam gives a survey of his own developing understanding of the issues of realism in 'Realismo e senso comune', in Mario De Caro e Maurizio Ferraris (eds), *Bentornata realtà: il nuovo realismo in discussione* (Turin: Einaudi, 2012), pp. 5–20.

The issue is the interpretation of Wittgenstein, and in particular one that is more open to a realist reading of 'forms of life' than Rorty's own pragmatism and apparent scepticism. Since it is generally taken that vocabularies are incommensurable, Rorty's argument is that there is no room left for realism.[12]

Cavell and Putnam differ from each other to the extent that Cavell does not seem as concerned as Putnam to defend a fundamentally cognitive account; indeed he defends a kind of scepticism.[13] But he certainly resists the line taken by Rorty. Cavell believes that the limitations of our knowing are simply our human condition; just as human is the continual resistance we have to accepting our ultimately limited position as knowers. We have to learn to live with both our sense of alienation and the need to acknowledge how things and others are; the mistake is to see it as a problem ('scepticism'). But the ways of living (our forms of life) that we have are the best we have got. In a telling observation he points out that our difficulty in knowing another person is not the traditional problem of 'other minds'; it is the obtuseness of our hearts that obscures our sensibility.[14] Cavell is happy to leave things as they are, and for us to live with our

---

[12]Áine Mahon, *The Ironist and the Romantic: Reading Richard Rorty and Stanley Cavell* (London: Bloomsbury 2014), pp. 3–4, distinguishes Cavell's interest in scepticism from Rorty's, with some references to Putnam.

[13]James Conant, 'Two varieties of skepticism', in Abel Günter and James Conant (eds), *Rethinking Epistemology*, vol. 2 (Berlin: Walter de Gruyter, 2012), pp. 1–73.

[14]Stanley Cavell, *The Claim of Reason: Wittgenstein, Skepticism, Morality, and Tragedy* (Oxford: Oxford University Press, 1979), p. 90, and esp. pp. 439–40; Stanley Cavell, *In Quest of the Ordinary: Lines of Skepticism and Romanticism* (Chicago: University of Chicago Press, 1994), p. 173. Giles Fraser discusses Cavell in ch. 5 of *Redeeming Nietzsche*, esp. pp. 156–7.

intuitions, however limited, and frustrating. Acknowledgement is fundamental, together with my ability to see the other person as me, what he calls 'empathetic projection'.

Cavell accepts the Wittgensteinian line that language goes all the way down. There is no non-linguistic knowledge.[15] But there is an intuition of what we are talking about. The idea of intuition belongs to a Kantian understanding that, although our knowledge is based on our conceptual understanding of appearances, and we have an intuition of what these are appearances of, we have no further cognitive grasp of reality. There is no pre-linguistic knowledge that can be used to *appraise* the effectiveness of a language. Cavell, then, understands the intuitive to go alongside the linguistic. As he puts it, using a turn of phrase from Emerson, 'no intuition without tuition' of concepts.[16] But, tellingly, he also speaks of an intimacy with the way the world is given us:

> Our relation to the world's existence is somehow closer than the ideas of believing and knowing are made to convey. What still wants expression is a sense that my relation to the existence of the world or to my existence in the world is not given in words but in silence.[17]

---

[15]See Stanley Bates, 'Skepticism and the interpretation of Wittgenstein', in Ted Cohen *et al.* (eds), *The Pursuits of Reason: Essays in Honour of Stanley Cavell* (Lubbock: Texas Tech University Press, 1993), pp. 225–40; see also Lynne Rudder Baker, 'On the very idea of a form of life', *Inquiry* 27 (1984), 277–89.
[16]Stanley Cavell, *Disowning Knowledge in Seven Plays of Shakespeare*, 2nd edn (Cambridge: Cambridge University Press, 2003), pp. 4–5.
[17]Stanley Cavell, *The Senses of Walden: An Expanded Edition* (Chicago: University of Chicago Press, 1992), p. 145.

Putnam, on the other hand, argues that Wittgenstein's account of language games gives us the appropriate form of knowledge, based on our ordinary engagements in human life. For Putnam, scepticism and metaphysical realism are two sides of the same coin. Wittgenstein is an answer to the problem of scepticism because he shows how it is based on a misconstrual of our cognitive position.[18] Putnam argues, with Wittgenstein, that in the end we have to trust something.[19] He refers to Cavell himself, and the positions are very close, but trust goes a bit further than Cavell's acknowledgement.

Cavell also, in fact, envisages our position as one that calls for more than acknowledgement. An indication of this is in his remark in *Disowning Knowledge* that an intuition that God is expressed in the world requires not evidence but understanding of a certain sort.[20] In the light of Wittgenstein's comments about knowledge, proof and reason, Cavell presumably has Kant's concept of understanding (*Verstand*) in mind rather than reason (*Vernunft*). And this is telling because he has elsewhere remarked how too much has been expected of certainty; things like information, skill and learning, the community dimension of knowledge, which

[18]Hilary Putnam, *Renewing Philosophy* (Cambridge, MA: Harvard University Press, 1992); see the essays collected in the section 'Wittgenstein: Pro & Con' in Hilary Putnam, *Philosophy in an Age of Science: Physics, Mathematics, and Skepticism*, edited by Mario De Caro and David MacArthur (Cambridge, MA: Harvard University Press, 2012).
[19]Putnam, *Renewing Philosophy*, pp. 177–8; Wittgenstein, *On Certainty*, §§508–9.
[20]Cavell, *Disowning Knowledge*, p. 3.

were part of the medieval and classical understanding of the
reasonable life, are overlooked.[21]

Wittgenstein refers to understanding in this sense, which
is learned and reflected on in a continuing process of growth
in knowledge. In *Culture and Value* he envisages that a person
might be brought up so as to be convinced that God exists; it
takes a certain kind of life. Indeed, for Wittgenstein, the whole
point of the cosmological kind of question ('Where does all
this come from?') is that it belongs to a certain kind of life,
expresses a certain kind of yearning (*Verlangen*).[22] This is the
context he gives for talking about thinking being grounded
in a 'picture or something else', or for the way there is a kind
of meaning that can only be described as 'gesticulating with
words', where what we are doing (*Praxis*) gives the words
their meaning.[23]

Contemplative epistemology

For me, this is an attractive way of talking about contemplative
experience. It is not a discursive state of reasoning. But it is an
awareness of our life, and of the way we find ourselves. It is

---

[21]Stanley Cavell, 'Avoidance of love: a reading of *King Lear*', in *Must We Mean
What We Say?* (Cambridge: Cambridge University Press, 1976), p. 323; see also
Stanley Cavell, 'The uncanniness of the ordinary', Tanner Lectures on Human
Values at Stanford University 1986, in *In Quest of the Ordinary*, pp. 153–78.
[22]Wittgenstein, *Culture and Value*, p. 85; contrast his ridicule of the idea at a
historical level in *Culture and Value*, p. 62.
[23]Wittgenstein, *Culture and Value*, pp. 83, 85.

engaged with and open to others. It underlies our thinking and we find it as we do because of the way we have been brought up to live. Acknowledgement and trust are fundamental to our ability to learn in this way of experience, as well as our ability to work with pictures, to gesticulate with words. The question about whether we should talk of it as a state of knowing or of scepticism somehow misses the point. Openness, and the readiness to let myself be disturbed by what I thought I knew, refusing to suppose that I am right, cultivating the habit, therefore, of being surprised by the ordinary rather than making judgements – these seem to be appropriate elements of the disposition. It is the reason why 'unknowing' seems an appropriate name for it.

There is a similarity here to the notion of wonder, which has had an established place in thinking about contemplation. For Aristotle it was a starting place for thinking, and for Plato it was a way of capturing the sense of the ultimate transcendence of truth from our capacities of understanding. The term can include not only the joyful, ecstatic experience of seeing what is nonetheless beyond our grasp, but also the darker, more painful experience of not being able to see or understand experience. A recent book aligns wonder with a range of states such as bewilderment and perplexity.[24] The closeness between wondering as an affective state in which

---

[24]Sophia Vasalou (ed.), *Practices of Wonder: Cross-Disciplinary Perspectives* (Eugene, OR: Pickwick, 2012), especially the discussion of Wittgenstein and Heidegger by Stephen Mulhall, 'Wonder, perplexity, sublimity: philosophy as the self-overcoming of self-exile in Heidegger and Wittgenstein', pp. 121–43.

propositional content is not in the epistemic foreground and the wonderings of questions, which have, at least implicitly, a more propositional structure, is instructive for the closeness between the non-cognitive and the cognitive elements in this basic state of experience where thinking starts. I would call it a non-discursive openness to truth, or to knowledge, but which is grounded in my affectivity. It is a notion that helps account for what goes on in threshold moments in liminal experience, where the sense of otherness and subjectivity plays with the recognition of a deeper kind of unity, a unity in relationship with otherness.

As already suggested, the experience can come across in different ways. Perhaps it is one where I feel taken up by something I cannot and do not try to understand into something greater, although in what I feel as a state of union I would retain my identity in as much as I am the knower of it. On the other hand, the contrary experience would work in a similar way; a situation where I feel crushed, negated as it were, by all that – but where I am still conscious of the overwhelming whole in relation to which I am struggling to find my identity and make sense. I think the range of 'nihilist' moments of boredom and less overwhelming sense of suffering, fit in the same matrix – and even moral ones of injustice, where my capacity to act intelligently is compromised.

The point of wonder is that it is a state where the emotional sense is given space for reflection and understanding. In a fine phrase, Wittgenstein speaks of philosophy's 'coolness'. A temple, providing a setting for the passions without meddling in them, is a good metaphor for contemplative experience.[25]

Faith and rationality

This account of epistemology is well suited to liminal experience. We cannot proceed cognitively, and the frustration of that is felt as alienation. The need for acceptance, for acknowledgement, is a precondition for any further progress, and that will involve trust. The shift of a limit to a threshold will be one where we are only able to gesticulate and point without being able to express meaning in the usual way.

Wittgenstein talks in *On Certainty* of the structure of belief as a scaffolding.[26] The scaffolding functions as a whole system of beliefs, a pattern of understanding into which we grow.[27] The propositions in the structure do not all have the same status.[28] In another image, of a riverbed shifting slowly with the flow of water, the structure is not static or rigid.[29] But as a whole they describe a 'world-picture', a 'mythology' even, itself a kind of

---

[25]Wittgenstein, *Culture and Value*, p. 2. The phrase is taken up by D. Z. Phillips, *Philosophy's Cool Place* (Ithaca, NY: Cornell University Press, 1999), to describe what he means by a contemplative approach to philosophy. See also Stephen Mulhall (in reply to him), 'Wittgenstein's temple: three styles of philosophical architecture', with Phillips' reply to Mulhall, both in Andy F. Sanders (ed.), *D. Z. Phillips' Contemplative Philosophy of Religion: Questions and Responses* (Farnham: Ashgate, 2007), pp. 13–27, 29–54.
[26]Wittgenstein, *On Certainty*, §211.
[27]Wittgenstein, *On Certainty*, §§141–2: 'Light dawns gradually.'
[28]Wittgenstein, *On Certainty*, §167.
[29]Wittgenstein, *On Certainty*, §§96–7.

language game that we learn how to play.[30] As we have noted, there is no rational ground to all this.[31] Explanation has to come to a stop somewhere, and Wittgenstein notes the difficulties that arise when we do not know where to stop, the danger of missing that we have reached the answer.[32]

In *Culture and Value* he gives the ideas a different twist. He says that we habitually fail to push our questions deep enough, right to the foundations (*Grund*) – there is no suggestion that this *Grund* is a matter of reason (*Vernunft*): he refers to where our thinking stops. He speaks of the difficulty of starting afresh, of the labour pain of thinking new concepts.[33]

Language tries to go on.[34] He talks about 'gesticulating with words', at the end of a section where he had spoken about what look like ordinary ways of talking 'in a deeper sense', of their being 'an expression of a certain yearning' (*Verlangen*: the English translation offers 'craving'), of an attitude that loses its seriousness because it is 'maintaining something more important'. Far from this being nonsense to be derided, Wittgenstein draws attention to how we use language to try to say more than what the words mean. That is his way of talking about a threshold. We cannot step outside or beyond it. We can

---

[30]Wittgenstein, *On Certainty*, §95; see also §167: a 'world-picture, not a hypothesis'.
[31]Wittgenstein, *On Certainty*, §166.
[32]This is the subject of D. Z. Phillips' essay, 'Wittgenstein's full stop', in *Wittgenstein and Religion* (Basingstoke: Macmillan, 1993), pp. 79–102, commenting on Wittgenstein, *Zettel*, §314; see also Ludwig Wittgenstein, *Philosophical Investigations*, translated by G. E. M. Anscombe, 3rd edn (Oxford: Blackwell, 1976), §1.
[33]Wittgenstein, *Culture and Value*, p. 62.
[34]Wittgenstein, *Culture and Value*, p. 85.

only play games on it, perhaps. At least it gives the particular context in which our language games take on their particular function at the limit of experience.

Wittgenstein goes on to say that life can educate a belief in God by experiences – not extraordinary ones, he explains – or by things that 'show us "the existence of this being"'. He seems to mean our ordinary experience of life; he singles out 'sufferings of various sorts', which in my account would be an example of something that takes us to the brink, to the limit of our understanding. Wittgenstein is interested in these experiences not because 'they give rise to conjectures about' God: as he says, 'Life can force this concept on us.' He does not say any more about the nature of religious language; he simply observes that if you want to stay within the religious sphere you must '*struggle*' (Wittgenstein's italics). He makes the comment after resisting the idea that a religious doctrine like divine judgement can be treated like a scientific hypothesis.[35] It harks back to the observations earlier about Christianity reading the Gospels not just as a straightforward historical narrative, and his comments there on doctrinal statements. As expressions of faith, they are believed 'though thick and thin, which you can only do as the result of a life'. As a narrative, 'you must make a quite different place in your life for it'.[36]

If we can take these remarks together with those in *On Certainty* about the grounding of the scaffolding of beliefs,

---

[35]Wittgenstein, *Culture and Value*, p. 86.
[36]Wittgenstein, *Culture and Value*, pp. 31–2.

we can construe the epistemology of faith in terms of a pattern of beliefs more basic than the propositions of history or scientific hypotheses, and which we come to believe as a whole. Its epistemological viability has to be seen in relation to contemplative experience, the way they express how we try to deal with our life, the *struggle* it takes. They express the liminality of experience as a threshold. He uses forceful language about our need for '*certainty*' (Wittgenstein's italics, again) 'and this certainty is faith'; it is 'what is needed by my heart, my soul, not my speculative intelligence. For it is my soul with its passions, as it were with its flesh and blood, that has to be saved.'[37]

This is a rationality of faith that makes sense of our acknowledgement of, and our trust in, contemplative experience. It is involved in the way my affectivity engages me, flesh and blood, with how I find myself called into question by my life. In doing so, it opens up not just faith but also hope and love, the other dimensions of contemplative living that were noted in the last chapter. Indeed, Wittgenstein goes further still to recognize the place of our passions. If the line of thought I have just been exploring from 1937 can be connected to his remarks at the end of *Culture and Value* (from 1950), the shift that opens up the threshold for faith, hope and love is one where the passions of 'sufferings of various sorts' turn to a passion for life, and, in particular, for a life that can live defiantly in the face of death.

In a response to the shocking news of the Asian tsunami in December 2004, Rowan Williams, then Archbishop of

---

[37]Wittgenstein, *Culture and Value*, p. 33.

Canterbury, touched on this kind of certainty, the religious motivation that stirred an enormous humanitarian response among people rather than disillusionment. He pointed out that the acknowledgement of faith, hope and love requires the ability to live with the paradox, that the 'immeasurable value, the preciousness, of each life' in a world that is freely given us is 'just what makes human disaster so appalling'. And yet this is what impels the urgency and generosity of response, even beyond available resources, that defies what most assaults that belief.[38] Contemplative prayer cultivates the necessary skills to take time with those questions at that depth and to try to feel more at home with its liminality and find a threshold of faith opening up.

Ways of unknowing

The epistemology suited to contemplative experience is better thought of in terms of unknowing than of knowing, the more so as our response to it is one of prayerful recognition of God's disclosing himself in the experience.[39] Contemplative experience is one where we try to cultivate a different kind of engagement with our experience from one where we are trying

---

[38]Rowan Williams, 'The Asian tsunami', *Sunday Telegraph* (2 January 2005), http://rowanwilliams.archbishopofcanterbury.org/articles.php/649/the-asian-tsunami (accessed on 15 October 2014).

[39]Besides *The Cloud of Unknowing* itself (in Spearing (trans.), *The Cloud of Unknowing and Other Works*), Martin Laird's *Into the Silent Land: The Practice of Contemplation* (London: Darton, Longman & Todd, 2006) and *A Sunlit Absence: Silence, Awareness, and Contemplation* (New York: Oxford University Press, 2011) are good treatments of the approach.

to take cognitive command of the situation. It is often prompted by our sense of not being able to do so. In these circumstances, we have to let things be, and, in our trying to be open to the strangeness of our position, our affectivity and subjectivity come more strongly into play. The last section argued that there is a particular kind of rationality involved in liminality at the frontier of thought, and it is suggested by the way that we continue to use language, albeit in a conative sense – as Wittgenstein puts it, 'gesticulating with words'. He also speaks of certainty, but of our passions, our affectivity and intuition, rather than of reason.

There are resonances here with the account that Pseudo-Dionysius gives of apophatic experience. The clearest is perhaps in the field of language, where he speaks of the frustration of our language, the inevitable use of oxymoron and paradox. But the conative dynamic of the passions and affectivity is also implicit in the movement he describes through the various levels of perception and intellectual knowing into the cloud, where we are led by love and desire. In contrast to modern discussions of apophasis which see it as acknowledging a boundary of language, beyond which is a silence that is cognitively impenetrable, Pseudo-Dionysius uses these linguistic techniques to try to spell out a cognitive space, a direction of meaning, beyond the normal ways in which we use such terms, for the knowledge of God even though no words can successfully articulate it. In the rest of this chapter I want to follow his lead in developing the idea of unknowing to open up the question of how contemplative experience could disclose itself similarly as a knowing of God.

There are differences as well as parallels. Pseudo-Dionysius took for granted the notion of intellectual transcendence beyond what was conceptually possible; a philosophy of the ordinary, where finitude sets the cognitive scene, cannot. And yet attitudes like acknowledgement or trust work in a similar way at the place of faith. The most considerable difference is that Pseudo-Dionysius moves in a metaphorical world where apophasis is described in terms of the ascent of a mountain, of an approach to God who, however, remains beyond view in material or conceptual terms. As in Plato, it is a dialectic process that leads someone on through the successive degrees of being, to the fundamental point where, in Christianity, the boundary between created and uncreated being is reached. The framework I have been working with moves more in a descent to a cognitive stalling point, of a different order, simply in virtue of the nature of language and its role in our intra-mundane experience.

In relation to what has been said previously, there are three 'moments' of unknowing we might notice. In the first place, in liminal experience my conceptual understanding is inadequate. It may be overwhelmed or undermined, but it is a situation I cannot handle conceptually; the handle breaks off! Second, the experience throws me into question: I don't know *where* I am, and I don't know where *I* am or even *who* I am.[40] The third moment is the way that I find myself confronted by the other in

---

[40]See Rowan Williams, '"Know thyself": what kind of an injunction?', in McGhee (ed.), *Philosophy, Religion and the Spiritual Life*, pp. 211–27.

a new way: the otherness of the situation forces me to engage with myself in a new way; I have to learn from this otherness a new way of being where I am, and so of my own understanding of myself. The shift in thinking is to recognize or acknowledge that something new is presenting itself, as something that takes me beyond the limits of my understanding, but which, I suggested, can disclose itself as a personal otherness that I recognize grounds my own sense of subjectivity.

For someone like Stanley Cavell, this is where the possibility of transcendence arises in human experience too, but for him it is a recurrent part of the human problem. At this point, where we also find ourselves struggling with language, paradox and images, we might find ourselves asking how this is to be understood in relation to the finitude of our experience. Is that all that can be said? I want to consider a possible way forwards from here.

The limit of experience and the recognition of God

A threshold in experience is a place of creative thinking; where explanation comes to a stop, thinking has to find a new beginning. It involves the imagination.[41] This means that no hard and fast lines can be drawn between 'realism' and

---

[41]Ronald W. Hepburn, 'Religious imagination', in McGhee (ed.), *Philosophy, Religion and the Spiritual Life*, pp. 127–43.

'idealism'. It is hard to tell the difference between discovery and invention, the two sides of the Latin verb *invenire*.[42] Poetry has been a regular companion for those trying to respond to liminal experience. Poetry's experimental use of language, sound, rhythm and image helps to educate our sensibility to imagine and understand things we could not otherwise put into words. It makes perfect sense that the later Heidegger became increasingly interested in the resources that poetry offered for exploring the frontiers of experience.

But more is needed than just the imagination to think out new possibilities of meaning. To make sense of a threshold and of what is beyond, we need some way of opening up a logical space for the imagination to work. This is where the logic of riddles might suggest a way forward. A stimulating discussion of this is in Cora Diamond's essay on Anselm's ontological 'proof' in the *Proslogion*.[43] She draws on a couple of comments in Wittgenstein's *Zettel*, which indicate in the abstract world of mathematical thinking that the solutions to problems, and discoveries, are about stimulating the imagination rather than about 'following rules'. Only in the light of the discovery do we understand the proof. So, in the case of riddles, she shows that we cannot follow the rule that is suggested by the grammar of the puzzle.[44] It can also be a moment of creative intelligence.

---

[42]Donald M. MacKinnon, 'The presidential address. Idealism and realism: an old controversy renewed', *Proceedings of the Aristotelian Society* 77 (1976), 1–14.
[43]Cora Diamond, 'Riddles and Anselm's riddle', in *The Realistic Spirit: Wittgenstein, Philosophy and the Mind* (Cambridge, MA: MIT Press, 1991), pp. 267–89.
[44]Wittgenstein, *Zettel*, §§696–7.

Riddles invite a way of answering them. For example: What has six legs, two heads and a tail? Answer: A man on a horse. The grammar suggests the answer is an individual, but a shift in thinking is called for. The sphinx's question to Oedipus about a creature with four legs, two and three, depends on an insight into the use of the word 'leg'. But lateral thinking to stimulate new insights is not the only thing. Diamond points to what happens with kissing; the child can respond appropriately to kissing a person, kissing the hand; with kissing toes, it will try to respond accordingly. A procedure is being applied. But kissing the ear? Perhaps the request is met by kissing the hand and touching the ear. The procedure cannot be followed, but the child adapts it appropriately; we laugh at the creativity of thought.

Solving riddles calls for a 'kind of groping search' for 'something not specifiable in advance, and which perhaps is not for anything that can intelligibly be described at all'. Diamond's point is that, at the frontiers, we cannot rely on a method. We can only know a good answer when we see one. But what the observer 'sees' is a response to something that is not there to be seen, but which is nonetheless waiting to be discovered.

Diamond refers to Wittgenstein's *Philosophical Remarks*.[45] Wittgenstein argues that a question can only be understood in terms of the method that is implied to answer it. Without such a method there is no problem, or question in the proper sense or in consequence, in the strict sense, any search for meaning. But

---

[45]Ludwig Wittgenstein, *Philosophical Remarks*, edited by R. Rhees (Oxford: Blackwell, 1975), §149.

he accepts that a new meaning or sense can be given, perhaps stumbled on, as a kind of 'revelation'. It would be like 'guessing' a riddle, as he puts it in *Philosophical Investigations*, and which he cites as a kind of language game.[46]

Wittgenstein refers to riddles in *Tractatus Logico-Philosophicus* as well. He speaks here of the 'riddle of this present life', the 'riddle *par excellence*'.[47] The point is that (according to the criteria of the *Tractatus*), since the answer cannot be put into words, the riddle does not exist. The 'solution' (his word) of the 'riddle of life in space and time lies *outside* space and time'. It is presumably part of the 'mystical' with which he ends the section.[48] Diamond calls this sort of thing a 'great riddle'. It marks a fundamental frontier of thinking. The remark 'It is not *how* things are in the world that is mystical, but *that* it exists' is famous; more apposite still to the theme of finitude that has been touched on is this from the following paragraph: 'Feeling the world as a limited whole – it is this that is the mystical.'[49]

Diamond argues that Anselm's proof might be interpreted in this light. His definite description 'that than which nothing greater can be conceived' can be interpreted similarly to the riddle question 'what is . . . ?'. The grammar invites a procedure,

---

[46]Wittgenstein, *Philosophical Investigations*, §23.

[47]Ludwig Wittgenstein, *Tractatus Logico-Philosophicus* (London: Routledge & Kegan Paul, 1961), §6.4312; Ludwig Wittgenstein, *Letters to C. K. Ogden with Comments on the English Translation of the Tractatus Logico-Philosophicus*, edited by G. H. von Wright and C. K. Ogden (Oxford: Blackwell, 1973), p. 37.

[48]Wittgenstein, *Tractatus Logico-Philosophicus*, §6.44; see also §6.52: the solution of all scientific questions will leave the problems of life untouched.

[49]Wittgenstein, *Tractatus Logico-Philosophicus*, §6.45.

but nothing can, in fact, be so conceived, as it will fall short of some hypothetical greater thing. Diamond draws a parallel with the oddity of the grammar in 'the last...'. We know how to talk about the last day in February, or the last day of the year, the last day of one's life, but not about the 'last day' *simpliciter*. The epistemological problem betrays a logical one. In these cases, we do not readily know how to apply the grammar to answer the question 'What is...?'.

Diamond's proposal is that these expressions have a 'promissory meaning'. That is to say, Anselm is happy to identify the solution of the 'riddle' of 'What is that than which nothing greater can be conceived?' with God, but on the basis of the fact that he believes in God and has therefore an independent route to the answer, although it is one that does not follow the method implied by the grammar of the question. The fool who denies the existence of God, however, must simply assert that the riddle is nonsense; for him, logically, there is no answer. As an analogy, Diamond likens it to the kind of question 'What is the next prime number after 47?' Answer: 53. The correct solution, however, is not reached, as the question seems to suggest, by a formula for answering the question; it can only be established by a painstaking examination of the intervening numbers. But 53 (the right answer) invites further reflection on the nature of prime numbers. It has a 'promissory meaning' supporting hope of a mathematical discovery in the future.

Similarly, then, in Diamond's argument, the hiddenness of God resembles the solution of a riddle. We have no idea what the solution will be like until we find it. People arrive at their belief in God by different paths, just as Anselm did. But we can only understand the religious character of belief within the grammatical horizon that these riddling expressions spell out. They open up a grammatical space for a conception of how reality may be greater than the whole of which we are conceptually aware. The religious language games that use this grammar in various ways help those who accept it to find their way around something that is, in any other way, beyond our understanding. In this kind of way, a structure for engaging with the possibility of transcendence can be conceived.

Diamond's discussion of riddles is important because she suggests a way of understanding the logical basis of what is acknowledged in contemplative prayer even though the normal logic of language and knowing breaks down. A later discussion of hers helps to develop the proposal.[50] It is largely a detailed exegesis of Wittgenstein's *Lectures on Religious Belief*, in which she tries, in particular, to reconstruct the exchanges with Smythies over the way pictures function in religious belief.[51] The crux is where Smythies protests that more is involved than a picture – as if religious beliefs were an expression of attitudes or just products of human imagination. Wittgenstein objects that 'the whole weight may be in the picture'.[52] The point is

---

[50]Cora Diamond, 'Wittgenstein on religious belief: the gulfs between us', in Phillips and von der Ruhr (eds), *Religion and Wittgenstein's Legacy* (Aldershot: Ashgate, 2005), pp. 99–138. These are the papers of the Claremont Symposium held in 2000.

[51]The issue is addressed in a slightly different way by Putnam in *Renewing Philosophy*, pp. 154–7.

[52]Ludwig Wittgenstein, *Lectures and Conversations on Aesthetics, Psychology and Religious Belief*, edited by Cyril Barrett (Oxford: Blackwell, 1966), pp. 71–2.

similar to his comments in *Culture and Value*, that we reach a level where 'a picture or something else' stands at the root of all our thinking.[53] Wittgenstein argues in his *Lectures* that pictures function in a special way. They have a particular grammar. We see Michelangelo's picture of the creation of Adam, and understand the representation of his finger, indeed of the cloak in which he is wrapped, in terms of the language games (biblical and iconographic) that give them their sense. Wittgenstein points out that we understand God's having an eye, without asking about his eyebrow![54]

Diamond examines closely how a picture can be irreplaceable, how it might carry all the weight. Rather as in the case of the 'point of a game' being intelligible only within the game,[55] Diamond argues that a picture carries the whole weight in which people who use the picture cannot give an explanation without using the picture. To illustrate the point, Diamond refers to George Berkeley who responded to an objection from sceptics that, although grace is what Christianity is all about, the idea lacks the necessary clarity and distinctness. Berkeley's reply was that the sense and usage is given within the framework of Christian doctrine (the picture), which for the sceptic is what is in dispute. To appreciate the authority of such a picture, you have to look at people's lives and the way they are shaped by their belief.

Riddles are a form of paradox. Like the forms of language we find ourselves using at the limit of experience, they open

---

[53]Wittgenstein, *Culture and Value*, §83.
[54]Wittgenstein, *Lectures on Religious Belief*, pp. 63, 71.
[55]Wittgenstein, *Philosophical Investigations*, §§561–70.

up a logic of promissory meaning, the kind of meaning that can only be illustrated by things like pictures and stories. This is a possible way of explaining what Pseudo-Dionysius was also trying to explain in terms of apophasis, a logic of transcendence that gives God and religious discourse its distinctive meaning and reference. The question that cannot be settled in advance is whether or not there is something that can be understood as the answer to what a person may be searching for in this kind of way. However, as Wittgenstein observed, it is not a question of finding the answer, but of an answer giving itself to be found. It is a matter of what he called 'revelation'.

In the same discussion Diamond uses an example which suggests how this idea of revelation might be understood. It is the story of Henry James meeting George Eliot, and recognizing how 'that magnificently ugly woman gives a totally transformed meaning to beauty'.[56] Applying the example to the present discussion: James can have a very clear sense of the logic of beauty (as with Anselm's ontological concept, it belongs to the language of perfection); it opens up an aesthetic space in which a person might be seeking the most beautiful girl in the world. There is promissory meaning. But only George Eliot could show James what the real meaning of beauty was, in concrete terms. She revealed it to him in a way contrary to any expectation.

---

[56]Cora Diamond, 'Wittgenstein on religious belief', pp. 125–6, referring to the American author's letters.

Conclusion

The argument only goes so far. But it can provide a basis for understanding the place of the Gospel story and the decisive moment of faith as our recognition of Jesus as the fulfilment of its promissory meaning. It certainly makes clear how the kind of contemplative awareness that underlies such a discovery is not a 'common core' kind of experience of transcendence; it is determined by the specific form of Christian teaching about the faith. But it does not yet explain how the kind of contemplative awareness that has been described very much in terms of human finitude can nonetheless be a point of transcendence, or how prayer can be understood in terms of a direct and personal encounter with God in his mercy and love even in the finitude of our human being.

This has to be the matter of the next chapter, but, before leaving this one, it is worth summarizing what it has tried to accomplish. Starting from the position that nihilism is a place where people find themselves looking at themselves in relation to life in ways that present the challenge or the invitation to faith or to spiritual growth and renewal of life, the response to nihilism by continental writers and philosophers suggested a kind of framework for understanding the structure of experience where the idea of a shift from limit to threshold offered a paradigm for thinking about the idea of an encounter with God, who necessarily lies 'beyond' the field of experience.

The epistemological reflections of this chapter offer a way of thinking about the logic of what is involved in the shift to a threshold where the notion of transcendence, of how 'beyond' the limit might be acknowledged, and also how it might be a place where God is known.

In developing the account in this way, I have emphasized the theme of finitude, which naturally puts all the more of a question mark against the notion of transcendence. And I have also, more briefly, suggested that our recognition of the importance of transcendence in relation to the riddles and pictures of religious language games is critically affected by our encounter with the person of Jesus, or of something that, in whatever way, brings the whole thing to life, and makes what is only of promissory meaning something that is real and active in determining how I live.

6

Being and Beyond

How, then, does God come in? Developing what was proposed in the last chapter, we can say that the encounter with Jesus is fundamental. Just as Henry James' encounter with George Eliot was a moment of revelation about the way beauty could be realized in a human being, our encounter with Jesus is the point that reveals the reality of God. He is the person who brings the logic of transcendence that has been hitherto a matter of riddles and paradox to life. The meaning of it all is what we learn from the preaching and life of the historical Christian community; that functions like the picture that carries all the weight. The incarnation is fundamental to Christian ontology, not only in that it reveals the Trinitarian ground for all being in the relation of creator and creatures, but also because it grounds the possibility of our engagement with God in the personal exchange of knowledge and love that is the heart of contemplative prayer.[1]

---

[1] I owe a great deal to two articles by Rowan Williams: 'Trinity and ontology', in *On Christian Theology* (Oxford: Blackwell, 2000), pp. 148–66, and 'The deflections of desire: negative theology in Trinitarian disclosure', in Oliver Davies and Denys Turner (eds), *Silence and the Word: Negative Theology and Incarnation* (Cambridge: Cambridge University Press, 2002), pp. 115–35.

I want to call this a realist account, but this needs explanation. In a standard realist account it would be hard to bring God in without turning him into an object of some sort, or in some way making him part of the fabric of being, which would be close to what people have resisted as onto-theology. But realism can be given a broader sense. We see it in the distinction Wittgenstein made between realism and empiricism.[2] His appreciation of the complexity of our use of language does not entail non-realism or idealism, even if it tries to respect the enormously complex ways in which language uses words to say things. In this sense I take realism to mean that what makes a statement true is something about the way things are, rather than the way I talk about them or the interest I have in them. Fergus Kerr gives a good distinction between realism and idealism when he says that the basic insight of realism is that what exists is independent of its knowability, whereas idealism asserts that things only have the intelligibility we give them.[3]

Kerr's argument is actually that Wittgenstein helps us 'dissolve' the distinction. This may be a provocative way of putting it.[4] But he points to a passage in *Philosophical Remarks*

[2]'Not empiricism and yet realism in philosophy: that is the hardest thing': Ludwig Wittgenstein, *Remarks on the Foundations of Mathematics*, §325, cited by Cora Diamond, 'Realism and the realistic spirit', in *The Realistic Spirit*, pp. 39–72; see also D. Z. Phillips, 'What God himself cannot tell us: realism v. metaphysical realism', *Faith and Philosophy* 18 (2001), 483–500.
[3]Fergus Kerr, 'Idealism and realism: an old controversy dissolved', in Kenneth Surin (ed.), *Christ, Ethics and Tragedy: Essays in Honour of Donald MacKinnon* (Cambridge: Cambridge University Press, 1989), pp. 15–33, pp. 18, 26.
[4]Kerr's discussion has been challenged by Nicholas Lash, in 'Renewed, dissolved, remembered: MacKinnon and metaphysics', *New Blackfriars* 82 (2001), 486–98; and by H. O. Mounce, 'The end of metaphysics', *New Blackfriars* 86 (2005), 518–27.

where Wittgenstein observes that, in all the philosophical talk about reality, what gets left out is what it is really all about, what is obvious and given, our life and what makes it what it is (*das Eigentliche*).[5] There is so much here that one simply takes for granted, while at the same time trying to mark a 'world' off and express it linguistically. He goes on to note that the obviousness of the world is all that language can signify. But it can never actually put into words its fundamentally transitory character.[6] Wittgenstein is unwilling to take sides in the philosophical war between realism and idealism of the mid-twentieth century, but happy to think that we can talk about how things are in a realist kind of way. His main concern is for what we take for granted; above all, that we need to notice, as Kerr puts it, 'how we are in the world... to dissipate the illusion that language is a kind of picture of the world'.[7] This concern for what Heidegger calls our *Dasein* is, however, exactly what the present discussion is trying to understand in terms of the frontiers of experience and language.

The contemplative tradition, which developed in close association with Platonism, offered the possibility of a strong account of our transcendence of the finite. Transmitted into a Christian context, the doctrine of creation helped amplify

---

[5]Wittgenstein, *Philosophical Remarks*, §47; at §55 Wittgenstein refers to the adherents of 'Realism' and 'Idealism' who think they are able to say something definite about the way the world is. He is himself more hesitant. Here and in the following paragraphs I am paraphrasing the German edition, *Philosophische Bemerkungen*, vol. 2 of *Shriften* (Frankfurt: Suhrkamp, 1964).
[6]Wittgenstein, *Philosophical Remarks*, §54.
[7]Kerr, 'Idealism and realism', p. 23.

and deepen this understanding, and it is important to note that modern commentators no longer regard Augustine of Hippo or Thomas Aquinas as vulnerable to onto-theological errors over being. In terms of the doctrine of creation, transcendence was possible in terms of our ability to know God and to grow in a union of grace with him because creation expressed the mind of God in the nature and purpose of created beings. Nonetheless, on the basis of the approach taken so far, in which finitude is fundamental to the human experience of reality, the retrieval of this contribution to an understanding of contemplative prayer cannot take transcendence from finite to infinite for granted.

Creation is one of the 'pictures' we cannot do without, because they carry all the weight; so more needs to be said about how our finite existence can be thought of in this way as an experience of divine meaning and purpose. It is where analogy comes in. Before we move on, however, Wittgenstein makes an observation about transcendence in the section of *Philosophical Remarks* that Kerr was commenting on. Wittgenstein says that the world is necessarily something we try to transcend: 'What a person cannot and is unwilling to transcend would not be the world.'[8] The double negative is misleading. The context shows that he is not saying that we are necessarily transcending creatures in a Platonist sense; he has been saying we cannot stand out of our way of being in the world and, as it were, look at it from outside. We cannot get a kind of fly-in-the-corner-of-

---

[8]Wittgenstein, *Philosophical Remarks*, §47.

the-wall, 'photographic', view of things. That just tries to leave out the very way that we know it, by moving around in it and living. What we cannot get out of, what we take for granted, is the world. But our way of living and taking it in is a kind of transcendence. It is the transcendence of being people who know how to move intelligently around. This is to put a slant on the observation that Kerr does not give. But it will be relevant later on.

Language, reality and God

Charles Taylor distinguishes between two approaches to a theory of meaning.[9] The one more familiar to English speakers is based on a strongly designative theory of language. It is associated with Hobbes, Bacon and Descartes, and stems from the break that nominalism effected between language and the recognition of meaning stemming from a transcendent source, be it Platonic Forms or divine creation. It works in terms of truth conditions, which earns it the label of T-theory. Gottlob Frege and the modern logical tradition obviously exemplify this approach. The other was developed, especially in the context of Romanticism, thanks to the work of people like J. G. Herder, Alexander von Humboldt and Heidegger (the three 'patrons' behind Taylor's HHH theory).

---

[9]Charles Taylor, *Human Agency and Language: Philosophical Papers* (Cambridge: Cambridge University Press, 1985), chs 9 and 10; developed in essays in his later book, *Philosophical Arguments* (Cambridge, MA: Harvard University Press, 1995).

The importance of the latter approach is that it addresses the question of how we are to explain the designations our language makes, an issue taken for granted in the T-theory that becomes acute in religious language, where the issue of referring to God is not straightforward. As Taylor puts it, the question that stimulates the HHH approach is about the distinctively human capacity to endow sounds with meaning and to grasp them as talking about things. It is the question that repeatedly emerges in Wittgenstein's discussions about language. It is what distinguishes him from logical empiricists, that he can be understood to have been working in a realist rather than an anti-realist metaphysical tradition, but with an expressive understanding of language. Like Herder, Wittgenstein appreciates that language is the way in which we exercise and communicate our reflective awareness of the world in which we live.

Taylor draws attention to the way that language discloses the world and brings it to light; it does not just point things out but establishes relationships between the people who use it. Language is used in all sorts of ways to express different things and the different ways in which we engage with our lives in the world. There is also a constitutive dimension in language, in that some things are partly constituted by the fact that we put them into words. Our awareness of things is sometimes constituted by what we say; hierarchy, power and intimacy, which are all relational things, require common understandings created by language, and so become an essential part of our feelings, goals and social relations. Taylor also points out how some feelings need the conceptualization that only language can give. Language makes it possible to notice indignation rather than just anger, admiration rather than just love.[10]

An expressive understanding of language shows how language plays a formative role in our knowledge, while still acknowledging that truthfulness depends on the world we are talking about. The fact that I can identify a set of responses as panic or as love does not change the world except insofar as it changes the way I engage with it and the way I am able to enter into deeper relationships with others in it. It makes for a more intelligent way of living, one that brings deeper resources of being into play, enhancing my human ability to live truthfully. This is the realist assertion. Truth is a richer concept than just a matter of propositions and conditions in which they are true or not. It is something to live by, something to walk in and to live towards. We need to tell the truth; and we need to face the truth. It is something by which we are judged. This understanding of truthful living expresses a relationship to reality that is informed by religion, but it also informs it. It is an understanding of realism as a way of life where we are accountable at more than just a cognitive level, both morally and spiritually.

Language is not, then, to be set in opposition to things as the criterion between realism and idealism. Language (with language games in a broader sense) shapes reality in terms of enabling our more intelligent engagement with it and our

---

[10]Charles Taylor, *Human Agency and Language*, pp. 263–73.

ability to live a more human life. In relation to God, we need to understand what religious language and grammar are trying to express in terms of our experience. The realist view is that it is God with whom we have to do, and that it is not just a matter of language. If language is how we bring the meaning of the world to expression, and religion is an act of faith, it will be a case of situating God within a view of things where he can be acknowledged in the way outlined in the previous chapter. This is what makes our response to limit-threshold experience one of prayer, where God makes himself present to our hearts and minds.

To think about the reality of God, then, we should recognize the ways in which, as D. Z. Phillips says, our experience 'brings us to our knees' in prayer, or makes us hold out our hands, be it in praise, confession, thanksgiving, intercession or offering.[11] These uses of language express and contribute to a sense in which I find myself in a world that is beyond my control, that I am part of something greater even than everything as a whole, with whom I have to do, where I have to look for meaning that I cannot give to things, and in relation to whom I find the fullest sense of my own being. This can be a positive thing expressed in praise; it can be a protest, or recognition of need for help. Prayer puts us in relation to the way our experience brings us to the limits of understanding and where we need to go 'beyond' in acknowledging God.

---

[11]D. Z. Phillips, 'On not understanding God', in *Wittgenstein and Religion* (Basingstoke: Macmillan, 1993), pp. 153–70, esp. pp. 160–2.

Expressing the meaning of the beyond

We recognize this religious dimension not because we see anything, but because it has been opened up as a possible logical space thanks to pictures, or practices that carry the weight of such an understanding. In order to take the next step, and say how God comes into the account of reality, it is necessary to stay with the picture, as it were, and how it has been developed in Christian theology. The purpose in doing so is to let it open up our experience of limit-threshold in terms of an encounter with God as the Christian tradition understands it. We discover the logical space for transcendence in our engagement with the person of Jesus Christ in all the ways the Church makes that possible. The encounter with Jesus engages our whole sense of being in the world; it affects the meaning we find in anything. Faith sets up a new hermeneutic circle for understanding the world; it is not a matter of rational deduction or induction, but the act of faith has appropriate grounds for it in the discovery of Jesus and the sense he makes of experience. It is an intelligible act, and its intelligence and wisdom are shown in the virtue and holiness of life it makes possible in those who live it out to the full.

The Jesus we meet in preaching is not just a historical person. Wittgenstein saw that this was (almost) beside the point. 'Christianity is not based on a historical truth; rather it offers us a (historical) narrative and says: now believe!'[12]

---

[12]Wittgenstein, *Culture and Value*, p. 32: 'The historical accounts in the Gospels might, historically speaking, be demonstrably false, and yet belief would lose nothing by this.' Dostoevsky's preference for Christ over the truth is similar.

The preaching is historical, but the message is a divine truth whose authority is the difference it makes to life. Wittgenstein says what matters is that people 'seize on' the message, and glosses 'believingly' as 'lovingly'. D. Z. Phillips speaks similarly of 'cherishing' a belief as something that shows the importance religious beliefs have in a person's life as whole, something that qualifies the extent to which religious language games can be thought of as a world unto themselves.[13] They shape a whole life and a way of seeing everything as a whole.

It is a complex theological picture. To know Jesus, according to the preaching, is to know the Father and to receive a share in the Spirit that is 'poured out' as the culmination of the drama of his death and resurrection. That is the crudest summary of the Trinitarian reality of Jesus Christ. The intention is to note how believing in Jesus speaks about reality in terms of creation, as well as about my existence, and about how I find myself engaged in creation's destiny and hope. What has hitherto only been a possibility in the way we find ourselves in the world as a logic of transcendence is addressed by the message of the Gospel, and acquires a promissory meaning. It is important to respect the limit between philosophy and theology. But, at the same time, I think it is possible to reflect on how the theological understanding of this picture fits in terms of human being and experience.

---

[13]D. Z. Phillips, 'Religious beliefs and language games', in *Wittgenstein and Religion*, pp. 56–78, pp. 57, 67.

Looking back at Wittgenstein's observations in *Culture and Value*, as a person who saw the kind of point that I have been trying to unpack in these chapters, but who eschewed the committed believer's point of view, the issue here is what it is about the narrative that wins my faith, that seizes me; how does it speak *so strongly* to my heart and soul?[14] What difference does it make? How is it manifested in my life?[15]

Beyond is not somewhere else

'Beyond' is a misleading term. Popular expressions like 'beyond the veil', or ideas implicit in the contrast made by Jesus when he says that 'my kingdom is not of this world', suggest a spatial distinction between here and somewhere else, beyond here. The danger is to read these in terms of a metaphysical distinction between, say, orders of reality. Liminality and threshold do not have a spatial location. They are where thinking comes to a stop, or treads water. It depends on person and circumstances. So 'beyond' should not be conceived as anywhere else than where we find ourselves coming to a stop. To address the question in relation to finitude, we need to look at elements that push, as it were, at the boundaries. The suggestion is that they invite us to look further, over the horizon of where we find ourselves.

---

[14]Wittgenstein, *Culture and Value*, pp. 32, 33.
[15]Wittgenstein, *Culture and Value*, p. 85.

There is a paradox here, of course. In Stanley Cavell's sceptical outlook, for instance, this continual search for transcendence is ironical, tragic even, because it must be continually frustrated; as human beings we continually need to be brought back to the limits within which we find our lives. But my argument makes no claim that we discover anything infinite that *makes* the finite other than what it is; or that we find signs of the infinite in the way we experience the world. We need to see how our experience of finitude, which comes to a stop at its limit, also suggests a horizon where we can recognize our experience of limit as an encounter with the God whom Jesus reveals to us. The finitude of reality is acknowledged, but the claim is that Jesus shows its finite value in a deeper perspective, in relation to a horizon where God makes his presence felt. The search for transcendence is therefore not ironical.

The limitations of finitude

In the human experience of life, the particularity and significance of things is about how they bear on us, a relational matter. The finite world I experience is not a flat world of objective criteria and co-ordinates, but one of complex perspectives, where I see things in their individual particularity and relatedness, and in relation to the way I find myself in the world. The relatedness, the immediacy and the distances disclose perspectives and suggest horizons.

These take their measure from my point of view, my way of going about things. The question is, then, whether these perspectives lie within an ultimate horizon that encompasses my experience of everything. I take this for granted because that is just how I see things the way I do, because it is inherent in the way I find myself in the world. Such an ultimate horizon would be the difference between Cavellian scepticism and Christian faith.

I think there are a few aspects of experience that do point in this direction. One is the gratuity of something's happening to be just as it is. The immediacy of what makes it what it is, the *this*ness and *here*ness of something has an intensity of meaning where I feel the tension between its preciousness and its precariousness.[16] Its value is at odds with its evanescence. Both are aspects of its finitude, but they are at odds with each other. The contrary is also the case, for example in the gratuity of an act of violence that does irreparable damage to a person.

This brings to mind another aspect, the sense of ultimacy in experience. An event has a decisiveness that far outweighs the contingent circumstances in which it occurs. What happens makes a difference to me (or others) that can never be obliterated. What we do can have an ultimate value that goes beyond the immediacy of our thinking, judgement and action. Even an accident can have enduring ramifications. This

---

[16]The English coinage is prompted by Scotus' *haecceitas*, most famously appreciated by Gerard Manley Hopkins.

is an inevitable consequence of the directionality of time. Time is an experience that puts us under judgement; where we risk standing condemned. It is a dimension of experience where we can never be in control of the outcome of our actions, but must nevertheless take responsibility for them. It is in marked tension with our sense of freedom, the dynamics of hope and desire that motivate our choices.

In both these ways, there is a tension, between the threat of nothingness and the unlimited possibilities of being. The Heideggerian experience of fallenness (*Verfallen*) and inauthenticity struggles with the possibility of hope and transformation. But, for being to have all this possibility, we should sense a fundamental tension between being as a potential for fullness and nothingness. As Rowan Williams points out in his comparison of Karl Rahner and Hans Urs von Balthasar, being finds itself in our experience not only against a limitless nothingness but drawn into a sense of participation in the fullness of being.[17] This is a reminder of the importance of wonder, not as an experience of God or of the infinity of the Absolute as such, but as opening our hearts and minds up to finitude as a possibility – and promise – of being. It is another way in which our experience pushes against a limit in experience, where we are open to liminality. It is the place of faith, and our exploration of the paradoxes of being in prayer.

---

[17]See Rowan Williams, 'Balthasar, Rahner and the apprehension of being', *in Wrestling with Angels*, pp. 86–105.

Faith and the gift of being

The human dimension of the experience of reality is marked, then, by things like gratuity, ultimacy and hope. To my mind, they are ways in which my experience of being points me to a horizon where I find myself wondering about the value of everything as such. My sense is that this wondering is where religious faith, to use Wittgenstein's verb, 'grips'.

It is where faith that comes from knowing Jesus *assures* me of the gratuity of being as God's gift of being even in its fragility. Its fragility and yet its beauty depend not on the necessity of a self-caused being, but on the freedom of God's entering into personal relationship with human beings, in which I find my own freedom even as a finite being. The same God speaks of the possibility of being even where it is jeopardized and corroded by death; the God of being is also the redeemer and saviour; and in so much he assures us of hope and the promise of transformation and glory. That is to say, there is a convergence between at least these categories and what faith in Jesus Christ reveals as the Divine Trinity.

In *God without Being*, Jean-Luc Marion accepted Heidegger's critique of onto-theology but argued that, instead of metaphysics and the traditional idea of God as Being, the phenomenology of Christian faith presented God better in terms of Gift. Dominique Janicaud then criticized Marion's phenomenological argument because the account of experience that phenomenology traditionally sought should be independent of metaphysical or theological categories.[18] While Marion subsequently changed his view about the onto-theology implicit in traditional metaphysics, the objection to the 'theological turn' in his proposal (and in French phenomenology in general) is important because of the need to distinguish the account we give of the structure of human experience from the structure of foundational beliefs that we use to give ultimate meaning to our experience.

So, in referring above to the gratuity of God's gift of being in its ordinary human fragility, I want to acknowledge Janicaud's objection by making clear that the idea of gift belongs to the picture that faith gives us, with which we understand the experience of finitude. While I think that we can recognize a paradox in limit experience where a sense of 'beyond' presses in, the finitude is real. We cannot pass across; but in the pressure we recognize God's self-disclosure.

To my mind, it is important that Trinitarian faith does not take away the paradoxes in experience; but it does offer a way of understanding them. An objection against Christianity, for example, is that it cannot allow for the tragic dimension of human existence. And, in fact, to say that God created a world that is so shocking and in which evil thrives sharpens the

---

[18]Jean-Luc Marion, *God without Being*, translation of the 2nd edn (Chicago: University of Chicago Press, 1991); his recantation of the accusation of onto-theology in Aquinas is in Jean-Luc Marion, 'Thomas Aquinas and onto-theology', in Michael Kessler and Christian Shepherd (eds), *Mystics: Presence and Aporia* (Chicago: University of Chicago Press, 2003), pp. 38–74. The criticism of the theological turn, made originally in 1991, is by Dominique Janicaud: see his *Phenomenology and the 'Theological Turn': The French Debate* (New York: Fordham University Press, 2000).

difficulty rather than eases it! When Stanley Cavell speaks of the
continual frustration of our desire for transcendence, he is true
to that side of human reality – its tragic dimension where our
desire for freedom from doubt and liberation from mistrust are
so strong. The Christian story also offers the possibility of faith,
not knowledge, but a possible way of living fruitfully in regard
to it. It is faithful to tragedy, because, even if it speaks of hope
and justification, it does not diminish in any way the sting of
death and the haunting fear of nothingness that are the crux in
the story of Jesus. But the pattern of Trinitarian faith also speaks
(in Cavell's terms) of the extraordinary sense that this way of life
has, a sense that reaches out for the hope of glory that we can
only experience as a paradox. We know that its assurance is from
beyond, and that we depend on power that we cannot see except
in the weakness of Jesus. And yet we believe. It is all we can do.

Creation and analogy

God's reality does not depend on metaphysics. That he is the
ground of being is deeply ingrained in Christian thinking,
thanks to the doctrine of creation. The doctrine is crucial
because it ensures that any Christian thinking is able to draw
the necessary distinctions between God and created reality. But
the doctrine leaves the metaphysical relationship between God
and creator profoundly mysterious, denying the two natural
ways of portraying the relationship. The one is the image of
manufacture, as in the biblical image of the potter shaping

clay; the other is the idea of derived being, with its powerful Platonic pedigree.

Creation is one of the pictures whose expressive power comes from the story of Jesus, together with the other pictures of apocalyptic judgement and, importantly, new creation through redemption. It is story-telling rather than scientific – or historical – explanation. Cora Diamond commented on the risk of muddling pictures up with explanation, and this is particularly easy where the picture, of creation, looks like a causal explanation.[19] But, for all its being a picture, Wittgenstein's argument allows us to say that this is how things are. There is a level of experience where explanation comes to a stop, where we have to think in a different kind of way in order to say how it is. In that sense, this approach is a form of realism.

It is an act of faith; no one is rationally compelled to make it. But, for someone who does, any other account would not be the complete truth. Disagreements here exactly match that between Anselm and the fool. Faith is the recognition that the truth of God illuminates the whole picture, and shapes the whole of our discourse in terms of creation and the meaning that God gives to things.[20] That is how it comes naturally to speak of God as Being. The only way faith can support this claim is in terms of the whole discourse that it makes possible. By the same token, what distinguishes this from fideism is the fact that beliefs are justified as a whole by their overall

---

[19]Cora Diamond, 'Riddles and Anselm's riddle', in *The Realistic Spirit*, p. 282.
[20]See Wittgenstein, *On Certainty*, §141.

explanatory authority, as well as by the credibility and integrity of the person's life that is shaped by them.

Analogy is fundamental to the discourse about reality that faith enables, because it makes it possible for us to speak of the world and God in a single language, but not in virtue of any quasi-scientific, that is to say metaphysical, account of being. Different accounts of analogy have been given. Karl Barth launched his criticism of the 'analogy of being' in natural theology, against the imputed doctrine that God's being was the basis of the nature of creation, in virtue of which some true things might be said of God. In response, some writers, drawing on Aristotle and Wittgenstein, distinguished between 'proportional analogy' (said to be what Barth was criticizing) and 'analogy of judgement' (or 'attribution') which was innocent of that kind of metaphysics, and made analogy a merely semantic matter.[21] There has been much discussion about when the 'crime' was committed and by whom. More recently, the semantic approach has been been challenged on the grounds that it too needs metaphysical underpinning in terms of causation rather than ontology.[22]

Analogy belongs to the heuristic and inventive power of language. It is part of how we tell the truth. David Burrell's

[21]Herbert McCabe in his contribution to the Blackfriars edition of Thomas Aquinas, *Summa Theologiae*, vol. 3, 1a, 12–13, *Knowing and Naming God* (London: Eyre & Spottiswoode, 1964), pp. 106–7; David Burrell, *Analogy and Philosophical Language* (New Haven: Yale University Press, 1973); Ralph McInerny, *Aquinas and Analogy* (Washington, DC: CUA Press, 1996).
[22]Thomas Joseph White, *The Analogy of Being: Invention of the Antichrist or the Wisdom of God?* (Grand Rapids, MI: Eerdmans, 2010); Stephen A. Long, *Analogia Entis: On the Analogy of Being, Metaphysics and the Act of Faith* (Notre Dame, IN: University of Notre Dame Press, 2011).

study of analogy, which belongs to the semantic approach influenced by Wittgenstein's thinking about language, starts from the basis that there is no clean distinction between literal meaning as opposed to imagery. Metaphor and image belong to the ways we discover of telling the truth. But he argues for an important distinction between analogy and metaphor, on the grounds that we use metaphor to tell the truth about the world, and analogy to talk about language and the ways in which we use it to tell the truth. It is a second-order distinction. Thus the Bible and Christian tradition shape our imagination and give us the images we need to tell the story; they imply a metaphysics, so that the story can become the basis for an account of everything. As part of the former, we need metaphor and images; analogy belongs to our reflection on the way these apply to the world – it belongs to reflection about the structures implicit in this discourse for telling the truth.[23]

And analogy is important for prayer because of the way language educates a sensibility that naturally sees things in relation to God and knows how to cultivate the dispositions to do so. The heart of the person at prayer is trying to see the world with the eyes of faith from the horizon at which faith is most immediately engaged with God. It is in the heart's ability to turn its gaze thoughtfully and lovingly to the world where it comes to know God as the source of reality that it is able

---

[23]Nicholas Lash, 'Ideology, metaphor, and analogy', in Brian Hebblethwaite and Stewart Sutherland (eds), *The Philosophical Frontiers of Christian Theology: Essays Presented to D. M. MacKinnon* (Cambridge: Cambridge University Press, 1982), pp. 68–94.

mindfully to negotiate the places where thinking comes to a stop and still look to God as its hope and fulfilment. It is a prayer where the play of metaphor, paradox and oxymoron engage the heart with the riddle of it all, so that it reaches out silently to God.

Praying beyond words

However important a theory of analogy is for prayer as well as for theology, contemplative prayer moves away from the divine meaning reflected in the created order to seek God in himself, in his difference from creation and otherness of being. This is the apophatic movement of prayer, where we wonder at the strangeness of what our experience does not reveal, but of whose presence we are aware. It is the 'cloud' of Pseudo-Dionysius. The exegesis of apophaticism was considered in Chapter 2, and now it is possible better to appreciate the context in which his thinking can be understood.

Philosophical readings of Pseudo-Dionysius tend not to give proper attention to the liturgical context in which he needs to be read. The invocative language and rhetoric of prayer that was noted before, however, make this performative context clear. It is the language of worship, not an exercise in the semantics of negation. The negatives are part of the positive activity of worship and of the relationships worship brings about, where what people do together expresses their response to what God has done and is doing for them, in them and through them. We miss the point if the negatives are understood as suggesting the absence of God; the interplay of negative language and hyperbole is Pseudo-Dionysius' attempt to show how such a symbolic environment can be the threshold of a deeper experience of God's presence, of an encounter with him beyond the symbolic. The liturgy celebrates what God does to create the space within which people are able to stand and inhabit the dimension of faith, as more than a picture, as a living reality, where time is gathered together from the past into the present in order proleptically to celebrate its future culmination.

But, precisely here, contemplative prayer responds to the need for deconstruction of what is only a symbolic world, in order to appreciate the reality of what is represented 'beyond' it. Since the weight is in the picture, only in silence can that acknowledgement take place. Yes, all this speaks of God and his mighty works. It makes his presence or *parousia* felt, but in a real sense God is not here. In recognizing God's absence in that sense, prayer goes beyond all the promissory meaning to attend to my neediness, to the power of non-being in my experience – but within the faith that gives me hope of redemption and of transfiguration. Rowan Williams expresses an aspect of this in his essay on Vladimir Lossky and the apophatic tradition, when he speaks of the silence of apophatic prayer in terms of repentance: apophasis is not a move in a conceptual game; it calls for the metanoia of the whole person.[24]

---

[24]Rowan Williams, 'Lossky, *via negativa* and the foundations of theoogy', in *Wrestling with Angels*, pp. 1–24.

There is a semantic irony here. Apophasis can be linked not only to the negation of the verb 'to speak' (*-phanein*), but also to the standard verb for 'to reveal' (*apophainein*). Language, especially in its liturgical use, serves to create a place where God can reveal himself. But God does so on his own terms, in silence. Cavell used the idea in a different context when he said that our engagement with reality was too close for language. It is given in silence. Similarly, I have argued that we can justify a real sense of transcendence of the finite, not because we move beyond it, but because we can recognize the space beyond the threshold as the place where God reveals himself in our encounter with the other.

There is an intense intimacy in the way that this is acknowledged in contemplative prayer. But God is not a pussy-cat; he is a lion. Intimacy is something that exposes us relentlessly to the other. There are times of wooing but there are also times for all the passions of the interplay of power within personal relationship. It leaves a person at times deeply confused, and asking questions about themselves, as well as, at other times, wondering in gratitude at the unmerited grace of an encounter. This interpersonal relationship is what constitutes the subject. Rowan Williams talks of the 'dialectic nature of being a subject, the inescapable involvement of the self in desire for the other'.[25] Similarly in relation to God, I know myself in knowing how my desire and my ability to be myself take me out of myself not in relation to another finite

---

[25]Rowan Williams, '"Know thyself"', p. 213.

person, but to one of whom I have no independent knowledge apart from the faith I have in what Jesus Christ has revealed.

The symbolic world of the liturgy is important because it helps me find my place in relation to God. But God is not there. The knowing that is going on between me and God goes on at a different plane, at a purely personal level. The traditional phrase used by John Henry Newman, *cor ad cor loquitur* (heart speaks to heart), puts it almost as well as any. It is a matter of love rather than knowing by sight or conceptual knowledge. At a human level, it is a trope that people find themselves unable to put what they want to say into words, but that does not detract from their knowledge of each other, let alone argue for their mutual lack of awareness.[26] So, in relation to God, we cannot know the being of God. But we can form an understanding of reality that lets God's presence be felt, and his presence be recognized in everything. But ultimately it is a matter of a different *theoria* altogether – a contemplation of the heart in love.

Since Stanley Cavell's emphasis on finitude has been so important a part of this chapter, the comment made on his scepticism by Stephen Mulhall might be noted.[27] For Mulhall, Cavell fails fully to interrogate the ego's maddened and maddening desire to believe itself at the centre of things, and so fails fully to acknowledge either the world's independence of the self or the uttermost depths of the self's finitude. In

---

[26]The point is well put by Nicholas Lash, 'Ideology, metaphor, and analogy', pp. 84–5.
[27]Stephen Mulhall, *Stanley Cavell: Philosophy's Recounting of the Ordinary* (Oxford: Oxford University Press, 1994), p. 311.

the end, Mulhall feels, Cavell is unable to let go of himself to accept the possibility of transcendence as a liberating movement to life, not just as marking the tragic condition of human living.

The challenge for contemplative prayer is whether we can let go of ourselves in relation to the mystery of this reality.

7

Prayer of Love and Silence

It is time to reflect on prayer itself as a work of love and silence. I want to focus on thinking about the significance of silence in prayer, and how silence works in relation to language in terms of a theory of meaning and of knowing in the dimension of faith. This bears, I think, on something similar to a traditional distinction between asceticism and mysticism, used, for example, by Evagrius of Pontus, which came to acquire a central place in spiritual theology.

Language, faith and worship

Language expresses the world in which we find ourselves and the way we find ourselves within it. Language helps us to articulate the whole of the subject–object relationship within the world that is the object of our knowledge. Wittgenstein famously remarks at the end of the *Tractatus* that that whereof

we cannot speak we must pass over in silence.[1] Presumably he
had no intention, in saying so, beyond finishing that work; but
his later discussions of the limits of thought give the remark
a fuller resonance: in *Zettel*, we noted, there is a point where
we have to stop; the difficulty is that we do not notice we have
reached what we were looking for and fail to recognize it.[2]
Silence plays an essential part at this point precisely in giving a
person the mental space needed to look and see. As one needs
time in a gallery to look at a picture, the more it challenges our
assumptions about reality and invites us to see things in a new
way. We need time to let it teach us how to look, and to reflect
on how it works, how it shapes our imagination and brings
things into focus. Silence and looking cultivate sensibility.

Similarly, we need silence to take in the meaning of the
pictures that carry what Wittgenstein calls the whole weight. In
Christianity, this meaning is carried in various ways by the story
and witness of people to Jesus Christ, by the way reflection on that
has itself permitted the construction of more complex 'pictures'
central to Christian doctrine (as well as the more fundamental
dogmatic 'rules' for reading or understanding them). There is also
the tradition of story-telling, and the various testimonies we have
as to how the story has been received and understood. All this
involves a complex hermeneutic, but by means of it we are able to
use the Christian story as a prism for reading our experience of
the world and the people around us. Prayer gives space for this.

---

[1]Wittgenstein, *Tractatus Logico-Philosophicus*, §7.
[2]Wittgenstein, *Zettel*, §314.

The importance of it as a context for understanding, and also for grounding and supporting a good life of prayer was expressed by Baron von Hügel when he noted that the 'mystical element' in religion needed to be kept in a healthy balance with both the institutional and the intellectual sides of religion.

This is what makes liturgical worship so important for the Christian contemplative tradition. It was recognized in earlier centuries when the Church was called the school of Jesus Christ. The bishop stood at the centre of the people of Christ and taught with the Word of God, alive and active in the world. The whole liturgical experience is understood as an encounter with the risen Christ. To make this accessible to believers, the Christian liturgy, together with the traditions of architectural space and iconography, tries to create a sense of sacred space and time, and to educate people in the rituals by which we keep the story alive as well as participate in it and find life thereby. The reality of the Church is realized most immediately in this liturgical environment. It is an 'academy of attentiveness', where our imagination is shaped perceptually in the understanding of this reality so that we are able to see our lives and experience more truly in relation to God in faith and prayer.[3]

Contemplative prayer cannot be understood apart from the context of Christian worship. Although its practice has generally become detached from liturgical celebrations, its historical and theological home is in the places of silence in the liturgy;

---

[3]See Nicholas Lash, 'Thinking, attending, praying', in John Cornwell and Michael McGhee (eds), *Philosophers and God: At the Frontiers of Faith and Reason* (London: Continuum, 2009), pp. 44–5.

deriving from this is the appreciation of sacred space as a place of prayer outside, but in relation to, times of common worship. Monasteries, for example, understood how sacred space and time could be extended over the whole of a way of life, so that the monastic enclosure was defined in relation to the church or oratory, the working day and night were defined by regular times of liturgical prayer, and the most important secular moments in the day were given rituals, above all at mealtimes, to wed them to the formal worship of the liturgy. In this encompassing sacralization of the environment, a person could learn to pray at all times and, especially through the practice of silence, learn to live a whole life contemplatively, continually nourished by and in response to the celebration of the story of faith.

The language of Christian faith creates a world that does not just exist in privileged liturgical spaces or at set times. Like the temple in Heidegger's reflections on the work of art, the architecture and rituals of Christian worship organize a whole world. Even for those who give up on the practice of faith, the church in the village green by the pub can still be an important sign of a dimension of life.[4] As an account of the whole of reality, the language games of faith are not just liturgical rituals, but use ordinary human rituals such as washing, sharing meals or laying on hands to spell out their ability to point beyond the mundane. The ordinary ways in which we relate to each other and communicate the meaning of human being in ordinary life can speak of God.

---

[4]The enduring significance of the English parish church even for non-practitioners of Christianity was well highlighted by Simon Jenkins in *England's Thousand Best Churches* (London: Allen Lane, 1999).

Silence is needed to take it all in, and to let 'it' make sense of a life in relation to God. We need the space of silence perhaps because the formality of liturgical ritual needs to be entered into and made one's own; conversely, the sheer ordinariness of an action or a situation may need time to unfold its sacred meaning in relation to the story of faith. Bridging the gap between faith and ordinary lives has been one of the purposes of traditional practices of meditation, especially in the medieval practice of *lectio divina*. For the reasons noted in Chapter 2, meditation or contemplation peeled off from the Bible and, as is sometimes seen in contemporary practice, became more about 'mindfulness' as a kind of psychological hygiene. It was easy to forget that meditation needs to be embedded in the intuitions of Christian faith and knowledge of Jesus Christ that are inculcated, above all, through the Bible. The revival of *lectio divina* in recent years has therefore proved especially helpful in enabling people to reflect on the Bible and on God's meaning in their daily lives. This can lead to a renewal of a life of prayer.

The point of the liturgy

Jean-Yves Lacoste recognizes the centrality of the liturgy as a locus for our encounter with God and makes it central to an account of Christian experience.[5] Working with Heidegger's

---

[5]Jean-Yves Lacoste, *Experience and the Absolute: Disputed Questions on the Humanity of Man* (New York: Fordham University Press, 2004).

approach to *Dasein*, which has played an important part in the thinking of this book, Lacoste notes the limitations in Heidegger's analysis of human being. He argues that the liturgy subverts Heidegger's phenomenological structure of *Dasein* as being-towards-death and creates an alternative environment where human being can find itself before God. Being-towards-death allows no relationship with the Absolute, and Heidegger's interest in the Fourfold and the loss of the dimension of the sky and divinity from human experience offers only an immanent sense of presence, and in no way engages with the transcendent. The liturgy, however, offers a setting where human being can experience the Absolute as wholly other, and it is in relation to the other that, I have suggested, we can find our own personal being.

But how is this liturgical encounter with God to be understood? What makes it more than just a drama? Is it something that the liturgy makes possible or is it something to which the liturgy bears witness? My own approach has been to see the liturgy as bearing witness to the meaning of the reality we discover prior to our engaging with liturgical structures of experience. It lies in the faith we discover before we go into church. The phenomenological basis of faith is about the liminality of experience of being, as such. The finitude of human existence, and our being-towards-death is fundamental to our ability to recognize God in an act of faith in response to the story of Jesus that is proclaimed. We participate in worship to illuminate and reimagine the story of our life with the hope of transfiguration it promises. The liturgy works by anticipating the ultimate meaning of finite being that faith opens up by creating a symbolic threshold for the encounter with God offered by the resources of the pictures of judgement and apocalypse to which Jesus himself appealed in his life and teaching.

That is clear, but prior to that is the recognition of the nothingness and finitude of our human existence, and of the need for faith. There is a liturgical celebration of this, and Lacoste discusses it tellingly in terms of the experience of the night vigil, where we wait empty-handed for the new light of day. There are also some important paragraphs devoted to the discussion of passivity in prayer, a kenotic moment of outpouring of a person's existence, yielding oneself completely to God's grace. But the tradition of the praying in the night vigil is a symbolic celebration of the liminality of human experience that has its home outside the liturgy; we explore it for its own sake in contemplative prayer. Indeed, a lot of what Lacoste says about liturgical experience rings true as a general account of contemplative prayer, which is how I think we actually live out our experience of liminality as waiting for God in faith and hope. This is why I want to turn to the part that silence plays in shaping our subjectivity.

Silence and subjectivity

Silence plays an important part in educating a person's subjectivity. Prayer engages me in the long process of inner reformation of mind, heart and spirit. At the level of my mind, the work is one of letting go of the way past memories grip or overshadow my attention, avoiding letting my mind run away to anxieties or concerns in the future; it is the patient work of continually bringing my mind back to the present and just letting things be. Good perception goes with not jumping too quickly to conclusions, but being able to withhold judgement. In the course of doing so, however, it is possible for me to begin to understand not just what attracts or distracts me, but how I am attracted and distracted, where it gets me. It is a way of learning not just about my relatively fragile attentiveness, but also something about my heart, the affectivity and moodiness that have so much to do with the way I engage with things. Silence gives me the personal space I need to pay attention to this, and to try to engage with experience more mindfully. It helps me grow in attentiveness. It is the beginning of a very long, but necessary, process that leads to what is traditionally portrayed as the vision of God.

The heart too needs reformation. The traditional language is purity of heart, which is a kind of transparency of motive and sensibility. Prayer involves moods, emotions, both passionate and more considered, as well as desires that motivate my subjectivity. Silence shapes my heart by helping me listen to the deeper thoughts that lie behind my inattentiveness. I have to address the preoccupations and habits of thinking that need to be recognized and befriended if they are to be set free – or if I am to be able to focus their desire on God. Part of this means recognizing my needs and dependencies – and finding some degree of freedom in relation to them; finally, it helps me understand and simplify my desire, a transformation which in turn reshapes my love. I think desire and love need to be brought into a strong relationship with each other, because love involves much more than desire, and crucially involves a selflessness in desiring, desiring the good of another not because of any interest or desire I have in that good, but because it is the good of the other.

Part of the problem, though, is that we sometimes do not know how we feel. It is not a straightforward thing. We need to listen to ourselves, and recognize the feeling. It is not a question of explaining it, just of identifying it. Often we are clumsy about our emotions, failing to pay them enough attention, or letting the passion direct our response before we really appreciate the situation. 'Emotional intelligence' needs refinement if we are to be good listeners or good at responding to situations. Eugene Gendlin's techniques of 'focusing', for example, are aimed at helping people create a sense of emotional space within themselves where they can tune into their subjectivity more perceptively.[6] It is fundamentally a matter of learning to listen. To do so, we often need to learn techniques, using images or symbols in order to work dialectically with sensations and desires that cannot yet be expressed in words until the mood or issue can come more clearly into focus. But the heart of the process is learning to give patient attention to ourselves and to make the space needed to listen.

---

[6]For example, Eugene T. Gendlin, *Focusing* (New York: Bantam Books, 1982).

Silence as listening

The reformation of spirit is something that comes about by finding the freedom of heart we need to let ourselves go in relation to God. The silence of prayer is for listening, listening to what is beyond our knowing on the threshold of experience, but God's presence is something that makes itself known in our own awareness of being, in particular in our awareness of how our being depends on its sense of being in relation to the other. Here silence reaches beyond understanding, and the way understanding is shaped by faith. Silence reaches out from the threshold of experience to the 'beyond'. Listening is the essential means by which this sense of relationship at the heart of our sense of identity grows. The faith and hope I have already spoken about in relation to worship turns to love.

It is a commonplace that we learn to pray with words; prayers and religious language games teach us the grammar of prayer; in contemplative prayer we learn how they put us into a relationship with God, with the reality that we engage with on the threshold of experience, which develops in silence. Here, silence goes beyond language and explores meaning that can only be expressed in the halting, inchoative, even paradoxical ways we find in mystical literature.

There are good and bad listeners; keeping silence is a virtue, which comes with practice, and it requires other virtues to flourish. It belongs, in other words, to a morally coherent life; in particular, it is an important part of a life where we learn how to live unselfishly and to prefer the concerns and interests of others to our own. Intellectual virtues are also involved, in so far as we need the right kind of balance between interest and disinterestedness, between a passion for truth, goodness and beauty and a dispassionate lack of concern about ourselves. Contemplative attention requires a particular sensibility on the part of the subject, but one that is as far as possible 'decentred', unattached to 'my point of view'. In Buddhist writing a great deal is made about the loss of subjective identity. But this should probably be understood not in relation to any idea of attaining the goal of mystical prayer; we have already seen that it is more probably to be understood in relation to the need for compassion and unselfish mindfulness.[7]

The virtues of selflessness enable us to give ourselves to one another in silence. Listening to another in silence demands actively giving attention, distinct both from speaking and from not speaking. We permit communication between each other by giving space to the other and by opening up possibilities for relationship and so for mutual presence, for people to be there for each other as persons. It lets the person be because we offer another the openness of our own attention as a space for them. The most important thing is, therefore, not the words or the capacity to hear, but the mutuality of the presence. Good listening includes hearing what remains unspoken, what sometimes cannot be said, but which needs recognition and reverence. It is the ability to catch the echo of what is said or

---

[7]Paul Williams, 'Non-conceptuality, critical reasoning and religious experience', esp. p. 204.

not said in the heart, or within the personal relationship that is open to the other. It involves honour and courtesy, almost more than understanding, where the other person can feel accepted and be given a voice with which to speak.[8]

The communicative dynamics of silence in listening teach us that silence is not another kind of language; it works in a complementary way to language, and goes beyond it, in that it enables meaning and communication to start. It also shows that, while it cannot replace language, silence takes us beyond a transactional understanding of the relationship, where language functions as a kind of currency of meaning exchanged between individuals. Properly understood, silence offers the possibility of a creative and also a potentially recreative and transformative experience where we can find ourselves in relationship to the other with or without language. Communion mediates and promotes experience. This is the way in which I think we should consider the value of silence in relation to the mutual presence practised in contemplative prayer in relation to God.

Listening to silence

Silence is not, therefore, just a space where I clear away distractions in order to be more attentive, or where I can sort out the deeper goings-on in my heart, so that I can be less

---

[8]A valuable study of this approach to silence by a Quaker, Rachel Muers, is her *Keeping God's Silence: Towards a Theological Ethics of Communication* (Oxford: Blackwell, 2004).

egoistic. It is a relationship, or the possibility of a relationship, with God who discloses himself where my experience runs out of words to express it. Initially, it may be something that hits me when I run into a limit experience, which can be profoundly disorientating and alienating. But it can become something I enter into, the more so as I recognize in that silence the possibility of relationship beyond all the particular relationships I have with others, thanks to which I am able to be more fully myself than I otherwise know how to be.

A picture that gives an idea of what goes on is that of a parent and child, or it could be any similar formative relationship. Children are restless and impetuous. The parent has to calm them before they can listen in any real sense; but this is something the parent has to facilitate rather than bring about. The parent has to *let* them calm down. 'Modelling' the desired calm enables it; but for it to work they need to feel secure and supported; they have to know they do not need to demand attention. They can let go of any anxiety of not being acknowledged. The picture shows how silence promotes change, and, above all, it promotes mutual presence. Between two adults, as in the previous section, the communicative dynamics of silence can go further in what they communicate to each other by their mutual presence.

As an analogy for thinking about prayer, these images suggest how silence helps us enter into a relationship with the otherness of God that can be meaningful beyond any words that are used to express it. Words are important for our sake; but their role is pragmatic; they stabilize and promote my understanding of, and so my continuing engagement in, the relationship I have with God. But in itself the relationship is hardly to be understood in the usual way as linguistically grounded. It goes deeper than language. This is consistent with what was said about language on the threshold of experience.

The relationship that we have with God in prayer promotes the continued and deepening process of purification. If silence is about mutual presence, it works by means of personal change. Heidegger's notion of 'attunement' (*Stimmung*) seems a good one here, as it can be recast in terms of reattunement or retuning. Typically, the physical senses, which play such a preponderant role in our giving attention and our vulnerability to distraction, are 'retuned' by silence; solitude and darkness play important roles, as well as physical techniques of sitting, kneeling or standing. It is not just a matter of deprivation, but also of harmonization, of working for a physical equilibrium – not because that is a precondition of prayer (think of Jesus' prayer in Gethsemane or on the cross!), but because it promotes attentiveness to what is unfamiliar.

Silence also promotes emotional retuning. In line with what has already been mentioned about distractions, silence restrains the immediate satisfaction of desires, and they are quick to come to the surface! The more immediate ones give way to the deeper desires that have a more pervasive influence on a person's attitudes and prejudices – on our choices, behaviour and character. The work we have to do here must address things that bear significantly on our capacity for relationship, in particular our self-absorption, vanity and pride. They interfere with a proper recognition of the other as such, independently of our personal interests in them. The problem is the stronger in relation to God who, as Nietzsche appreciated, so easily becomes a projection of our own needs and desires.

But the deepest change is at the level of our spirit, where our sense of personal identity is found in our relationship, 'in the Spirit', with God. This kind of 'transfigurative praxis' is promoted by silence.[9] It lets us grow more familiar with the way we are supported even on the threshold of experience and where we engage with the mystery of existence and find ourselves engaged there by the otherness whom we acknowledge as God, and in whose presence we can receive ourselves back in love. Cavell's word, 'acknowledgement', is a good one. It is not a cognitive act in the sense of a conceptual judgement about what I perceive. But in the experience I have of myself in relation to what is completely other, I find myself engaged; it is a personal response that invites me into relationship. It is not so much a matter of conceptual knowledge as of the personal knowledge of love. The knowing grows out of that, and is informed by the pictures and revelation of faith that enable understanding and imagination. The interdependence of personal relationship is important here. It is what promotes 'self-critical vigilance'; it is a means of change through repentance.[10]

---

[9]Peter Hodgson, *God in History*, quoted by Rowan Williams, 'Hegel and the gods of modernity', in *Wrestling with Angels*, pp. 25–34, p. 31.

[10]See Williams, 'Hegel and the gods of modernity', p. 33; repentance is also glossed as '*metanoia* of the whole human person' in Williams, 'Lossky, the *via negativa* and the foundations of theology', p. 2.

In relation to God, silence enables a radical simplification of desire. An unreflective life wants all sorts of things and can scarcely distinguish between more or less important wants where there is no space to be aware of them. Silence, and the emotional stability that comes from being able to sit still and keep silence, gives a better chance to notice the differences, let us say, between needs and desires, between drives and more reasonably grounded priorities and plans. They all have their respective importance, but prayer is even more about letting desire of a more fundamental kind come forward. It does so to the extent that our desiring has found its fulfilment, even a fulfilment different from or beyond what we had expected. The curious thing about real desire is that it is never satisfied, but the restlessness of the heart that has found its fulfilment is one that does not need to cast around for different things to entertain it. The heart has found its love, its treasure. Even when God is not endlessly interesting, the purer or simpler the heart, the clearer is its sense that nothing else will do. No other enables it to desire as much.

This brings in the erotic dimension of existence to the contemplative life. As silence simplifies the heart and unifies desire, that core energy comes into its own as a fundamental human desire to give life, and to make it in giving it. Plato's attention to Eros in the dialogues that became central to the Christian mystical tradition is no accident, even though his intellectualism seems to make the distinguishing of 'true' (spiritual or intellectual) Eros from the lesser, carnal type a bit schematic. It is an aspect of human being that is absent from

Heidegger's model of being-towards-death. But, if we accept the sense of personal affirmation in intersubjectivity, we can begin to appreciate that life is something we are given and therefore to be lived in giving. The desire to give ourselves is, however, extremely costly – 'costing not less than everything', as T. S. Eliot says. We therefore avoid facing up to this desire, 'owning' it (in the modern sense), at any rate until we can trust, or take the risk of trusting – it is a matter of taking a risk, to give our life away.

The gift of ourselves is the gift of love that truly responds to the sense we have of being loved, and it is in this giving that is mutual giving that we can try to understand the idea of union that is the goal of Christian prayer. But it is also the paradox of prayer that I shy away from the risk and the cost of what most of all promises life!

Mysticism and union with God

Implicit in the account just ventured is a twofold process that is similar to the traditional distinction in the Christian tradition, for example in Evagrius of Pontus, between ascesis (or *praktike*) and the contemplative mysticism of *theoretike*. The ascetic element is what I have talked about in terms of our learning to appropriate the understanding of faith so as to make it the principle of a way of life, and let it shape our hearts; the other element is the engagement with God that this makes possible, not only by means of the liturgy, where the concept of the mystery of faith is rooted, and in the extension of it in personal practices of prayer, but especially in the silent engagement with God on the threshold of experience, where our desiring is simplified and purified in love and by love.

The account differs from the traditional one because, instead of envisaging the soul's ability cognitively to pass beyond the finitude of human existence into higher realms of being, contemplative prayer is the way we acknowledge God's presence over the threshold of experience, as the one whom we meet in faith and hope thanks to the story of Jesus Christ. But this is consistent with what I understand Pseudo-Dionysius to say about *apophasis*, even though he worked within a Christian-Platonic ontology. Contemplative prayer, accordingly, lets the whole Trinitarian reality disclosed by Jesus' birth, death and life beyond death in resurrection unfold, not just in our understanding, but in our lives, so that we become more and more part of that mystery of life and let it transform us so that its hope is able to give meaning to the world. Listening to the word we hear in the Bible, and celebrating it in the liturgy is how we grow in the love of the Father manifest in the Son by the power of the Spirit, which he pours out in our hearts.

The mystical vision that is granted us is nothing out of this world; it is the ability to see the extraordinary in the ordinary. This is Cavell's way of putting it but with a sense he did not give it. It is to see the possibility of a reality and a future where death is transformed by love. It is to let the mystery of Christ illuminate our vision of the world and become the reality in which we find ourselves and in which we live and move and have our being. We learn to see how we are caught up in the creative, redeeming, transforming power of God; how our life is renewed by the Spirit that lives by giving itself away.

This is how we should make sense of the traditional idea of union with God. It contrasts with an approach that sees union as an intellectual identification of the knower with the object of knowledge, a model that, in its original Greek home, involved seeing the Form or essence of something. The approach has influenced ideas about the beatific vision and the possibility even in this life of a mystical vision of God's essence or (in the Greek tradition) his uncreated light.

One of the attractions of Heidegger's approach to being as a historical reality is the scope it gives to the eschatological nature of being. In *Being and Time*, Heidegger understands being as being-towards-death, in an ontological relationship with nothing. Not only does the Christian story redeem that understanding of being and give it a different perspective, but the story of Jesus' death and resurrection seems the more vital for engaging directly and immediately with the truth of our being-towards-death and representing it (within the act of faith) as disclosing the glory of its destiny. Christian hope springs from that disclosure to faith, and transforms the life that remains as it was before, bound to death, but no longer held by the fear of its power. The Christian mystery, therefore, is bound to the paradox that the pouring out of one's life even unto death, even the frustration of love rejected and apparently wasted, is the ground of glory. Kenosis and transfiguration belong to the eschatological hope of Christian faith.

The account that I am giving of mysticism is, therefore, one in which our union with God is lived out in costly Christian love for our fellow human beings, in which we show the meaning of the lives we ourselves live because of what we have discovered in Jesus Christ. It is a life of communion with him; he lives in us by the Holy Spirit. That is another way of putting it. But it is what we act out liturgically in the Eucharist.

A Eucharistic model of union is a far cry from the loss of identity and subjectivity that is sometimes found in other religious texts. It is not a matter of losing either in any ontological sense. If I am living a life of radical love, I have to let go of the concerns to protect myself or my identity, to define myself against others. Rather, I discover the need to let the other person define me! In so far as my attention is directed unreservedly to others, or to God, I will not be aware of myself, of course. But that is not to say I have lost my identity. I am devoting it to others.

In Christian tradition there is another tradition of thinking about union in spousal terms, of a mystical union between the human being and Christ, on the model of that spoken of in the Bible between God and his people, or between Christ and the Church. This develops the Eucharistic model of union in terms of the intimacy of relationship enjoyed in prayer between a believer and Jesus Christ. It also corresponds to the erotic dimension of desire that is an important mode in terms of which we can conceive of our knowing God on the threshold of experience.

Erotic union is one where we each find ourselves in the other, and the mutuality of relationship is at the heart of what is enjoyed. A less intense image that works in a similar way is the dance where the two partners, and there may be more, move continually in relationship to each other and to others, enjoying the exchange of initiatives each takes in the course of the music, interpreting it by their movement. This image of union has the added value of being more spacious, open and responsive to others, even while, as is often the case, the dance works in partnerships. Not to be overlooked either is the way the idea of dance implicit in the Greek word *perichoresis* has been used in thinking about the relationships between Father, Son and Spirit in the Trinity. This is the ultimate context within which the life of contemplative prayer has to be understood, as our participation in the mystery of the Trinity whose self-giving and transfiguring love has been disclosed to us in Jesus Christ.

CONCLUSION

Contemplative prayer springs from the roots of our human being, and the way we find ourselves in the world. I have tried to tease out how this can be appreciated by seeing prayer in relation to the underlying structure of our experience of being. It is something I have come to appreciate even more strongly as I have worked on this book. It also expresses the conviction that our heart's restlessness finds its peace in our orientation towards God; prayer is the expression of our faith and hope in him, the expression of our love in response to his. This mutual gift of love is how our humanity grows to its full enjoyment of life in the gift of the Spirit who brings us to life in Jesus Christ.

That is the promise of prayer, but that way of putting it overlooks the real *difficulty* of prayer. It puts God securely in the grammar of a sentence, who is, in practice, continually elusive and challenging to the very faith that drives our search for him. We will always be embarrassed by the precariousness of our humanity; by the suspicion of hearts that are slow to believe; by our anxiety in the face of our dependence on what we can never possess; by the fact that we are loved into being, even when the reassurance we find in that often seems overshadowed by the challenge of meeting its demand.

The original motivation of this book was an attempt to respond to a particular experience of this elusiveness. It is a very different book from the one that I thought needed to be written several years ago, because the disorientation I described in the Introduction seemed to me so similar to the kind of alienation that underlies the literature I have appealed to in the early part of this study. I have called it 'nihilism', which is a widely used term; it is misleading because it is a label more for where people have found themselves, rather than for the way in which they have tried to make sense of their lives. To be sure, for many it has included a rejection of religious faith; but it has also prompted a different kind of search for God, one that has been followed more in the shadows of human subjectivity and experience than in the open ground of reason.

What is instructive is the way that kind of search has taken people to the frontiers of experience, where we need to recognize the limitations of reason and conceptual thinking – not that faith is irrational (though that is how it has seemed to some working in the territory) but that thought and reasoning shift when they reach that kind of limit.

There are a number of responses to this nihilism, and I admit that in Christianity one has been to reassert the very tradition that has been challenged, and to do so on the grounds that it has been misunderstood in the way it has been received by modernity. I do not venture to disagree with this approach. I have simply tried to outline an alternative, which someone like myself, whose experience has been completely shaped by modernity (for all my classical education), might still find accessible as a way of thinking in particular about prayer. In doing so, I have tried to find my own footing, as it were, as

someone who certainly wants to believe and who tries to pray.
On this ground, I would like to think that the basic truthfulness
and wisdom of the earlier tradition can also be appreciated. It
is a tradition I love and to which I owe so much that continues
to give me life.

So I have tried to do something different in this book. I have
tried to look at the contemplative tradition in a postmodern
context, though it has also been an attempt to recover that
tradition from the more sceptical stances of postmodernism
against metaphysics, epistemology and personal subjectivity. It
has also tried to acknowledge the importance of the postmodern
critique of modernity and the way in which modernity has
distorted a proper reception of the pre-modern tradition.

I have tried to show how prayer springs from the point
where our conceptual thinking starts, at the very basis of
human experience. I started from the idea that even when
God seems most remote and absent, and prayer most unreal,
the heart of what is involved in prayer is disclosed. The
concrete finitude, the frustrations as well as the desires, hopes
and ambitions, of our life bring us to limits, which can seem a
brick wall but can become a threshold for opening our hearts
to a sense of a beyond. Everything I have tried to say about
prayer has been based on trying to make better sense of what
is going on at this point. The role of faith and, as I argued,
hope and love in our engagement with the experience of limit
is the critical thing.

In reflecting on this, I have used Wittgenstein a great deal, and
those who have developed his work. This is because I think his

exploration of the philosophical implications of faith is deeply instructive. He was acutely conscious of finitude and suspicious of the ways our thinking evades its implications in our attempts to get outside the actual fabric of our life. Traditional Christian faith, committed to belief in a transcendent God and in a human destiny beyond death, seems at odds with so much of his thinking. This makes the strength of his concern to understand it aright all the more significant.

There are several ways of reading Wittgenstein, and I have followed one that, while recognizing the significance of language games, is fundamentally more realist in orientation than the way some Wittgensteinians would read him. A great deal depends on the exegesis I have followed of Wittgenstein's discussion of pictures and of revelation at the point where thinking and explanation give out and rest simply on how we see things. Cora Diamond's work in this regard has been crucial.

Nietzsche and Heidegger have played such a large role because they are seminal writers for anyone engaging with the spirituality of our contemporary culture. They speak directly to the sense of alienation with which I started. The need to address the challenges that Nietzsche raises seems to me to be of the greatest importance, the more so as some ways of doing so in postmodernism seem to raise more questions than they answer. Heidegger has his own part to play in that story, and I have tried to engage with his approach to phenomenology in a different way, in order to retrieve the appreciation of experience that bears so much on the understanding of contemplative prayer.

The basic task, however, has been to try to tease out the implications of prayer, which seems to be, so much of the time, the experience of a blank, but to be an activity which for all the reasons I have for wanting to stop and get on with something more productive, more stimulating, I know I am the poorer for neglecting. Not that there is any way in which I am aware of the reward for sticking to the work of prayer, except that I know it raises my sensitivity and compassion for others; it helps me live more deeply in a sense of engagement with others and more appreciative of the extraordinary beauty and wonder that life has when I know how to look at it from a contemplative point of view.

I think this account of prayer leads to some new emphases in the way contemplative prayer is to be understood. I think it is able to explain what makes contemplative prayer in the Christian tradition different from prayer in another religious tradition. The connection between faith and prayer is fundamental because it is what makes the shift possible in the liminality of our experience of finitude to a sense of a threshold that opens up to what is beyond as the recognition of God. The threshold becomes the place of prayer where we engage with God in faith, hope and love. Here, it tries to explain the ambiguity of that threshold state, as one that we cannot cross, but where we are engaged by what is beyond, in terms of the dynamics of intersubjectivity in our relationship with God in prayer.

A further result of the account I have given is to have shown how contemplative prayer must be seen in close relationship to the life and worship of the Christian community. It is so often seen and practised as a solitary activity, and, without this sense of relationship, its connection with the sources of nourishment of Christian faith can become highly attenuated. Above all, I wanted to show the links between contemplative prayer and the Bible (*lectio divina*) as well the liturgy; they are the two ways in which the Christian tradition and the Christian community educate the sensibility we need to be able to see things, as it were, from God's point of view, and to see everything in relation to God.

By the same token, it follows that we can hardly find the fullness of life in contemplative prayer without being fully engaged in the life and witness of a local Christian community, whether that is a parish, a monastic or religious community or some fellowship in a school or place of work. The links between ethics and contemplation, or, for that matter, between contemplation and politics, are ones that there has, sadly, been no chance to follow through.

But I hope I have shown that the philosophical interest of contemplative prayer is more than just a theoretical one, or rather that the theory touches what it means to have life and to have it in abundance.

REFERENCES

Aquinas, Thomas, *Summa Theologiae*, Blackfriars edition, vol. 3, 1a, 12–13, *Knowing and Naming God*, edited by Herbert McCabe (London: Eyre & Spottiswoode, 1964).

Augustine, *Confessions*, edited by Maria Boulding and John E. Rotelle (Hyde Park, NY: New City Press, 1997).

Baker, Lynne Rudder, 'On the very idea of a form of life', *Inquiry* 27 (1984), 277–89.

Bates, Stanley, 'Skepticism and the interpretation of Wittgenstein', in Ted Cohen, Paul Guyer and Hilary Putnam (eds), *The Pursuits of Reason: Essays in Honour of Stanley Cavell* (Lubbock: Texas Tech University Press, 1993), pp. 225–40.

Brown, Malcolm, *Nietzsche Chronicle*, www.dartmouth. edu/~fnchron/1888.html (accessed 12 November 2014).

Bunge, Gabriel, *Earthen Vessels: The Practice of Personal Prayer According to the Patristic Tradition* (San Francisco: Ignatius Press, 2002).

Burrell, David, *Analogy and Philosophical Language* (New Haven: Yale University Press, 1973).

Calati, Benedetto, 'Western mysticism', *Downside Review* 98 (1980), 201–13.

Cassian, John, *Conferences*, edited by Boniface Ramsey, Ancient Christian Writers (Mahwah, NJ: Newman Press, 1997).

Cavell, Stanley, 'Avoidance of love: a reading of *King Lear*', in *Must We Mean What We Say?* (Cambridge: Cambridge University Press, 1976), pp. 267–353.

Cavell, Stanley, *The Claim of Reason: Wittgenstein, Skepticism, Morality, and Tragedy* (Oxford: Oxford University Press, 1979).

Cavell, Stanley, *Disowning Knowledge in Seven Plays of Shakespeare*, 2nd edn (Cambridge: Cambridge University Press, 2003).

Cavell, Stanley, *In Quest of the Ordinary: Lines of Skepticism and Romanticism* (Chicago: University of Chicago Press, 1994).

Cavell, Stanley, *The Senses of Walden: An Expanded Edition* (Chicago: University of Chicago Press, 1992).

Cavell, Stanley, 'The uncanniness of the ordinary', Tanner Lectures on Human Values at Stanford University 1986, in Stanley Cavell, *In Quest of the Ordinary: Lines of Skepticism and Romanticism*, pp. 153–80.

Chapman, John, *Spiritual Letters*, introduction by Sebastian Moore, OSB (London: Burns & Oates, 2003).

Coakley, Sarah, 'Dark contemplation and epistemic transformation: the analytic theologian re-meets Teresa of Avila', in Oliver D. Crisp and Michael C. Rea (eds), *Analytic Theology: New Essays in the Philosophy of Theology* (Oxford: Oxford University Press, 2009), pp. 280–312.

Coakley, Sarah, *Powers and Submissions: Spirituality, Philosophy and Gender* (Oxford: Blackwell, 2002).

Coakley, Sarah, 'Prayer as divine propulsion: an interview with Sarah Coakley', *The Other Journal: An Intersection of Theology and Culture*, part 1 (20 December 2012), http://theotherjournal.com/2012/12/20/prayer-as-divine-propulsion-an-interview-with-sarah-coakley/; part 2 (27 December 2012), http://theotherjournal.com/2012/12/27/prayer-as-divine-propulsion-an-interview-with-sarah-coakley-part-ii (accessed on 6 October 2014).

Coakley, Sarah, 'Traditions of spiritual guidance: Dom John Chapman OSB (1865–1933) on the meaning of "contemplation"', in *Powers and Submissions: Spirituality, Philosophy and Gender*, pp. 40–54.

Conant, James, 'Two varieties of skepticism', in Abel Günter and James Conant (eds), *Rethinking Epistemology*, vol. 2 (Berlin: Walter de Gruyter, 2012), pp. 1–73.

Cottingham, John, 'The spiritual and the philosophical quest: Augustine Baker and René Descartes', in Geoffrey Scott (ed.),

Dom Augustine Baker 1575–1641 (Leominster: Gracewing, 2012), pp. 153–78.

Davies, Brian, *An Introduction to the Philosophy of Religion*, 3rd edn (Oxford: Oxford University Press, 2003).

Diamond, Cora, 'Realism and the realistic spirit', in *The Realistic Spirit*, pp. 39–72.

Diamond, Cora, *The Realistic Spirit: Wittgenstein, Philosophy and the Mind* (Cambridge, MA: MIT Press, 1991).

Diamond, Cora, 'Riddles and Anselm's riddle', in *The Realistic Spirit*, pp. 267–89.

Diamond, Cora, 'Wittgenstein on religious belief: the gulfs between us', in D. Z. Phillips and Mario von der Ruhr (eds), *Religion and Wittgenstein's Legacy* (Aldershot: Ashgate, 2005), pp. 99–138.

Dreyfus, Hubert L. and Mark A. Wrathall (eds), *A Companion to Heidegger* (Oxford: Blackwell, 2005).

Gellman, Jerome, 'Mysticism and religious experience', in William Wainwright (ed.), *The Oxford Handbook of Philosophy of Religion* (New York: Oxford University Press, 2005), pp. 138–67.

Guigo II, *Ladder of Monks and Twelve Meditations*, edited by Edmund College and James Walsh (Kalamazoo, MI: Cistercian Publications, 1981).

Forman, Robert K. C., *The Innate Capacity: Mysticism, Psychology, and Philosophy* (Oxford: Oxford University Press, 1997).

Forman, Robert K. C., *Mysticism, Mind, Consciousness* (Albany: SUNY Press, 1999).

Forman, Robert K. C., *The Problem of Pure Consciousness* (Oxford: Oxford University Press, 1990).

Fraser, Giles, *Redeeming Nietzsche: On the Piety of Unbelief* (London: Routledge, 2002).

Gendlin, Eugene T., *Focusing* (New York: Bantam Books, 1982).

Guignon, Charles B. (ed.), *The Cambridge Companion to Heidegger*, 2nd edn (Cambridge: Cambridge University Press, 2006).

Hadot, Pierre, *Exercices spirituels et philosophie antique*, new edn (Paris: Albin Michel, 2002).

Hadot, Pierre, *Philosophy as a Way of Life* (Oxford: Blackwell, 1995).

Hardy, Alister, *Spiritual Nature of Man: A Study of Contemporary Religious Experience* (Oxford: Oxford University Press, 1979).

Heidegger, Martin, *Basic Writings*, edited by David K. Krell (London: Routledge & Kegan Paul, 1978).

Heidegger, Martin, *Contributions to Philosophy (Of the Event)*, translated by Richard Rojcewicz and Daniela Vallega-Neu (Bloomington: Indiana University Press, 2012).

Heidegger, Martin, *Discourse on Thinking: A Translation of 'Gelassenheit'*, by John M. Anderson and E. Hans Freund (New York: Harper & Row, 1966).

Heidegger, Martin, *Essere e tempo*, 3rd edn, edited and translated by Alfredo Marini (Milan: Mondadori, 2013).

Heidegger, Martin, *Nietzsche 1936–1953*, 4 vols, translated by David Farrell Krell (New York: Harper & Row, 1979–87).

Heidegger, Martin, *Off the Beaten Track*, edited and translated by Julian Young and Kenneth Haynes (Cambridge: Cambridge University Press, 2002).

Heidegger, Martin, *On Time and Being*, translated by Joan Stambaugh (New York: Harper & Row, 1972).

Heidegger, Martin, *Pathmarks*, edited by William McNeill (Cambridge: Cambridge University Press, 1998).

Heidegger, Martin, *What is Called Thinking?* (New York: Harper & Row, 1968).

Hepburn, Ronald W., 'Religious imagination', in Michael McGhee (ed.), *Philosophy, Religion and the Spiritual Life*, pp. 127–43.

Howells, Edward, 'Mysticism and the mystical: the current debate', *The Way Supplement* 102 (2001), 15–27.

Janicaud, Dominique, *Phenomenology and the 'Theological Turn': The French Debate* (New York: Fordham University Press, 2000).

Jenkins, Simon, *England's Thousand Best Churches* (London: Allen Lane, 1999).

Kant, Immanuel, *Critique of Pure Reason*, edited by Paul Guyer and Allen W. Wood (Cambridge: Cambridge University Press, 1998).

Katz, Stephen, *Mysticism and Language* (Oxford: Oxford University Press, 1992).

Katz, Stephen, *Mysticism and Philosophical Analysis* (London: Sheldon Press, 1978).

Katz, Stephen, *Mysticism and Religious Traditions* (Oxford: Oxford University Press, 1983).

Katz, Stephen, *Mysticism and Sacred Scripture* (New York: Oxford University Press, 2000).

Kerr, Fergus, 'Idealism and realism: an old controversy dissolved', in Kenneth Surin (ed.), *Christ, Ethics and Tragedy: Essays in Honour of Donald MacKinnon* (Cambridge: Cambridge University Press, 1989), pp. 15–33.

Kerr, Fergus, *Work on Oneself: Wittgenstein's Philosophical Psychology* (Washington, DC: Catholic University of America Press, 2008).

Kitaro, Nishida, *An Inquiry into the Good* [1911], translated by Masao Abe and Christopher Ives (New Haven: Yale University Press, 1990).

Lacoste, Jean-Yves, *Experience and the Absolute: Disputed Questions on the Humanity of Man* (New York: Fordham University Press, 2004).

Laird, Martin, *Into the Silent Land: The Practice of Contemplation* (London: Darton, Longman & Todd, 2006).

Laird, Martin, *A Sunlit Absence: Silence Awareness and Contemplation* (New York: Oxford University Press, 2011).

Lane, Belden C., *The Solace of Fierce Landscapes: Exploring Desert and Mountain Spirituality* (Oxford: Oxford University Press, 2007).

Lash, Nicholas, *Easter in Ordinary: Reflections on Christian Experience and the Knowledge of God* (London: SCM Press, 1988).

Lash, Nicholas, 'Ideology, metaphor, and analogy', in Brian
    Hebblethwaite and Stewart R. Sutherland (eds), *The
    Philosophical Frontiers of Christian Theology: Essays Presented
    to D. M. Mackinnon* (Cambridge: Cambridge University Press,
    1982), pp. 68–94.
Lash, Nicholas, 'Renewed, dissolved, remembered: MacKinnon
    and metaphysics', *New Blackfriars* 82 (2001), 486–98.
Lash, Nicholas, 'Thinking, attending, praying', in John Cornwell
    and Michael McGhee (eds), *Philosophers and God: At the
    Frontiers of Faith and Reason* (London: Continuum, 2009),
    pp. 39–50.
Liégeois, A., R. Burggraeve, M. Riemslagh and J. Corveleyn, '*After
    You!' Dialogical Ethics and the Pastoral Counselling Process*,
    Bibliotheca Ephemeridum Theologicarum Lovaniensium 258
    (Leuven: Peeters, 2013).
Lipari, L., 'The vocation of listening: the other side of dialogue', in
    A. Liégeois *et al.*, '*After You!*', pp. 15–36.
Long, Stephen A., *Analogia Entis: On the Analogy of Being,
    Metaphysics and the Act of Faith* (Notre Dame, IN: University
    of Notre Dame Press, 2011).
Louth, Andrew, *Origins of the Christian Mystical Tradition: From
    Plato to Denys*, 2nd edn (Oxford: Oxford University Press, 2007).
MacKinnon, Donald M., 'The presidential address. Idealism
    and realism: an old controversy renewed', *Proceedings of the
    Aristotelian Society* 77 (1976), 1–14.
Mahon, Áine, *The Ironist and the Romantic: Reading Richard
    Rorty and Stanley Cavell* (London: Bloomsbury, 2014).
Marion, Jean-Luc, *God without Being*, translation of the 2nd edn
    (Chicago: University of Chicago Press, 1991).
Marion, Jean-Luc, 'Thomas Aquinas and onto-theology', in
    Michael Kessler and Christian Shepherd (eds), *Mystics:
    Presence and Aporia* (Chicago: University of Chicago Press,
    2003), pp. 38–74.
McGhee, Michael (ed.), *Philosophy, Religion and the Spiritual
    Life*, Royal Institute of Philosophy Supplement 32 (1992).

McGinn, Bernard, *The Flowering of Mysticism: Men and Women in the New Mysticism (1200–1350)* (New York: Crossroad, 1998).

McGinn, Bernard, *The Foundations of Mysticism: Origins to the Fifth Century*, The Presence of God: A History of Western Christian Mysticism (New York: Crossroad, 1991).

McGinn, Bernard, *The Growth of Mysticism* (New York: Crossroad, 1994).

McGinn, Bernard, 'Quo vadis? Reflections on the current study of mysticism', *Christian Spirituality* 6: 1 (1998), 13–21.

McGinn, Bernard, review of Denys Turner's *Darkness of God*, *Journal of Religion* 77 (1997), 309–11.

McInerny, Ralph, *Aquinas and Analogy* (Washington, DC: CUA Press, 1996).

McIntyre, Alex, *Sovereignty of Joy: Nietzsche's Vision of Grand Politics* (Toronto: University of Toronto Press, 1997).

Merton, Thomas, *Contemplative Prayer* (London: Darton, Longman & Todd, 2005).

Merton, Thomas, *Zen and the Birds of Appetite* (New York: New Directions, 1968).

Moore, Sebastian, 'Some principles for an adequate theism', *Downside Review* 95 (1977), 201–13.

Mounce, H. O., 'The end of metaphysics', *New Blackfriars* 86 (2005), 518–27.

Muers, Rachel, *Keeping God's Silence: Towards a Theological Ethics of Communication* (Oxford: Blackwell, 2004).

Mulhall, Stephen, *Stanley Cavell: Philosophy's Recounting of the Ordinary* (Oxford: Oxford University Press, 1994).

Mulhall, Stephen, 'Wittgenstein's temple: three styles of philosophical architecture', in Andy F. Sanders (ed.), *D. Z. Phillips' Contemplative Philosophy of Religion: Questions and Responses* (Farnham: Ashgate, 2007), pp. 13–27.

Mulhall, Stephen, 'Wonder, perplexity, sublimity: philosophy as the self-overcoming of self-exile in Heidegger and Wittgenstein', in Sophia Vasalou (ed.), *Practices of Wonder*, pp. 121–43.

Nelstrop, Louise, with Kevin Magill and Bradley B. Onishi, *Christian Mysticism: An Introduction to Contemporary Theoretical Approaches* (Farnham: Ashgate, 2009).

Nietzsche, Friedrich, *The Gay Science*, edited by Bernard Williams, Cambridge Texts in the History of Philosophy (Cambridge: Cambridge University Press, 2001).

Phillips, D. Z., 'On not understanding God', in *Wittgenstein and Religion*, pp. 153–70.

Phillips, D. Z., *Philosophy's Cool Place* (Ithaca, NY: Cornell University Press, 1999).

Phillips, D. Z., 'Religious beliefs and language games', in *Wittgenstein and Religion*, pp. 56–78.

Phillips, D. Z., 'What God himself cannot tell us: realism v. metaphysical realism', *Faith and Philosophy* 18 (2001), 483–500.

Phillips, D. Z., *Wittgenstein and Religion* (Basingstoke: Macmillan, 1993).

Phillips, D. Z., 'Wittgenstein's full stop', in *Wittgenstein and Religion*, pp. 79–102.

Proudfoot, Wayne, *Religious Experience* (Berkeley: University of California Press, 1985).

Pseudo-Dionysius Areopagita, *De Coelesti Hierarchia, De Ecclesiastica Hierarchia, De Mystica Theologia, Epistulae*, Corpus Dionysiacum Band 2, Patristische Texte und Studien 36, edited by Günter Heil and Adolf M. Ritter (Berlin: Walter de Gruyter, 1991).

Pseudo-Dionysius, *The Complete Works*, Classics of Western Spirituality, translated by Colm Luibhéid and Paul Rorem (New York: Paulist Press, 1987).

Putnam, Hilary, *Philosophy in an Age of Science: Physics, Mathematics, and Skepticism*, edited by Mario De Caro and David MacArthur (Cambridge, MA: Harvard University Press, 2012).

Putnam, Hilary, 'Realismo e senso comune', in Mario De Caro and Maurizio Ferraris (eds), *Bentornata realtà: il nuovo realismo in discussione* (Turin: Einaudi, 2012), pp. 7–20.

Putnam, Hilary, *Renewing Philosophy* (Cambridge, MA: Harvard University Press, 1992).

Richardson, John, *Heidegger* (Abingdon: Routledge, 2012).

Riemslagh, M., 'Asymmetric reciprocity in pastoral dialogue: reflections on effective pastoral counselling inspired by the thought of Lévinas and Buber', in A. Liégeois *et al.*, *'After You!'*, pp. 139–58.

Robertson, Duncan, *Lectio Divina: The Mediaeval Experience of Reading* (Collegeville, MN: Liturgical Press, 2011).

Rorty, Richard, *Consequences of Pragmatism* (Minneapolis: University of Minnesota Press, 1982).

Sells, Michael A., *Mystical Languages of Unsaying* (Chicago: University of Chicago Press, 1994).

Spearing, A. C. (trans. with intro. and notes), *The Cloud of Unknowing and Other Works* (London: Penguin Books, 2001).

Studzinski, Raymond, OSB, *Reading to Live: The Evolving Practice of 'Lectio Divina'* (Collegeville, MN: Liturgical Press, 2009).

Suzuki, D. T., *The Zen Doctrine of No Mind* [1949] (New York: Weiser, 1991).

Swinburne, Richard, *The Existence of God*, 2nd edn (Oxford: Oxford University Press, 2004).

Taylor, Charles, *Human Agency and Language: Philosophical Papers* (Cambridge: Cambridge University Press, 1985).

Taylor, Charles, *Philosophical Arguments* (Cambridge, MA: Harvard University Press, 1995).

Turner, Denys, *Darkness of God: Negativity in Christian Mysticism* (Cambridge: Cambridge University Press, 1998).

Tyler, Peter, *The Return to the Mystical: Ludwig Wittgenstein, Teresa of Avila and the Christian Mystical Tradition* (London: Continuum, 2011).

Vasalou, Sophia (ed.), *Practices of Wonder: Cross-Disciplinary Perspectives* (Eugene, OR: Pickwick, 2012).

Weil, Simone, 'Reflections on the right use of school studies with a view to the love of God', in *Waiting on God*, translated by Emma Crauford (Glasgow: Collins, 1983), pp. 66–76.

White, Thomas Joseph, *The Analogy of Being: Invention of the Antichrist or the Wisdom of God?* (Grand Rapids, MI: Eerdmans, 2010).

Williams, Paul, 'Non-conceptuality, critical reasoning and religious experience: some Tibetan Buddhist discussions', in Michael McGhee (ed.), *Philosophy, Religion and the Spiritual Life*, pp. 189–210.

Williams, Rowan, 'Balthasar, Rahner and the apprehension of being', in *Wrestling with Angels*, pp. 86–105.

Williams, Rowan, 'Butler's Western mysticism: towards an assessment', *Downside Review* 102 (1984), 197–215.

Williams, Rowan, 'The deflections of desire: negative theology in Trinitarian disclosure', in Oliver Davies and Denys Turner (eds), *Silence and the Word: Negative Theology and Incarnation* (Cambridge: Cambridge University Press, 2002), pp. 115–35.

Williams, Rowan, *Dostoevsky: Language, Faith and Fiction* (London: Continuum, 2008).

Williams, Rowan, 'Hegel and the gods of modernity', in Rowan Williams, *Wrestling with Angels*, pp. 25–34.

Williams, Rowan, '"Know thyself": what kind of an injunction?' in Michael McGhee (ed.), *Philosophy, Religion and Spiritual Life*, pp. 211–27.

Williams, Rowan, 'Lossky, *via negativa* and the foundations of theology', in *Wrestling with Angels*, pp. 1–24.

Williams, Rowan, 'The Asian tsunami', *Sunday Telegraph* (2 January 2005), http://rowanwilliams.archbishopofcanterbury. org/articles.php/649/the-asian-tsunami (accessed 15 October 2014).

Williams, Rowan, '"Religious realism": on not quite agreeing with Don Cupitt', in *Wrestling with Angels*, pp. 228–54.

Williams, Rowan, 'Trinity and ontology', in *On Christian Theology* (Oxford: Blackwell, 2000), pp. 148–66.

Williams, Rowan, *Wrestling with Angels*, edited by Mike Higton (London: SCM Press, 2007).

Wittgenstein, Ludwig, *Culture and Value*, edited by G. H. von Wright (Oxford: Blackwell, 1980).

Wittgenstein, Ludwig, *Lectures and Conversations on Aesthetics, Psychology and Religious Belief*, edited by Cyril Barrett (Oxford: Blackwell, 1966).

Wittgenstein, Ludwig, *Letters to C. K. Ogden with Comments on the English Translation of the Tractatus Logico-Philosophicus*, edited by G. H. von Wright and C. K. Ogden (Oxford: Blackwell, 1973).

Wittgenstein, Ludwig, *On Certainty*, edited by G. E. M. Anscombe and George Henrik von Wright (Oxford: Blackwell, 1975).

Wittgenstein, Ludwig, *Philosophical Investigations*, translated by G. E. M. Anscombe, 3rd edn (Oxford: Blackwell, 1976).

Wittgenstein, Ludwig, *Philosophical Remarks*, edited by R. Rhees (Oxford: Blackwell, 1975). German edition: *Philosophischen Bemerkungen*, vol. 2 of *Shriften* (Frankfurt: Suhrkamp, 1964).

Wittgenstein, Ludwig, *Tractatus Logico-Philosophicus* (London: Routledge & Kegan Paul, 1961).

Wittgenstein, Ludwig, *Zettel*, 2nd edn (Oxford: Blackwell, 1991).

Wrathall, Mark A., *Heidegger and Unconcealment: Truth, Language and History* (Cambridge: Cambridge University Press, 2011).

Zupi, Massimiliano, *Incanto e incantesimo dire*, Studia Anselmiana 143 (Rome: Sant'Anselmo, 2007).

INDEX